THE LABOUR PARTY
IN TRANSITION
1931—1938

THE LABOUR PARTY
IN TRANSITION
1931—1938

By

DEAN E. McHENRY, Ph.D.,

Assistant Professor of Political Science,
Pennsylvania State College

LONDON
GEORGE ROUTLEDGE & SONS, LTD.
BROADWAY HOUSE : CARTER LANE, E.C.

First Published 1938

PRINTED IN GREAT BRITAIN BY HEADLEY BROTHERS
109 KINGSWAY, LONDON, W.C.2 ; AND ASHFORD, KENT

TABLE OF CONTENTS

PART III. THE PARTY IN ACTION

PART IV. TACTICS AND POLICIES

CONTENTS

PART V. CONCLUSION

PREFACE

In the life-history of a great political party there are five natural divisions or chapters : the first deals with its origin ; the second, with the period between organization and advent to power ; the third, with its experiences while in power ; the fourth with its experiences while in opposition ; the fifth, with the causes and circumstances of its dissolution.

A. D. MORSE, *Parties and Party Leaders*, p. 25.

THIS is a study of the structure and problems of the Labour Party from 1931 through 1937, a period of six years as His Majesty's Opposition in Parliament. The origin and growth of the Party have been sketched briefly in the introductory chapter. Primarily, however, I have been concerned with examining the Labour organization and its record since the General Election of 1931.

Americans of progressive leanings long have admired the British Labour Party rather overcreduously. Like many of my countrymen I have been curious about this Party which vaulted from a humble beginning to national office within a single generation. As a student of American Parties I was anxious to observe a major Party machine built without those twin evils of our politics, the spoils system and financing by the wealthy.

When the opportunity to investigate the Labour Party did come, I decided at the outset not to attempt any definitive history of the Party, but to confine my work to inventorying its resources and tracing its trends over a limited period. My study has been restricted further by personal inclinations—I am more interested in practical politics than in theoretical considerations. Therefore this book contains much on the structural, action side, but little on policies and tactics.

A foreigner, I approached this project with obvious disadvantages : my acquaintance with the subject had to be acquired over a brief period ; the risks of getting misinformation and of misinterpreting data were ever present. On the other hand, without claiming to be a " man from Mars ", an overseas investigator may enjoy certain advantages of detachment and objectivity; he receives fresh impressions and may be able to evaluate his findings in the light of comparative materials.

My wife and I moved to England for the year 1935-6. We set up housekeeping in London, joined the London Co-operative Society, and steeped ourselves in Labour lore. During the General Election campaign, we visited two dozen constituencies in different parts of the country. We interviewed Labour's opponents ranging from a Cabinet Minister in Downing Street to a Communist lady in Merthyr Tydfil. We stalked

Labour leaders in constituency and Parliament. We haunted London County Hall, Glasgow City Chambers and numerous town halls in search of data on Labour in local government. We reviewed with care the wealth of writings on the Labour Party, in books, periodicals, pamphlets, and leaflets.

It is impossible here to thank all the people who have aided in assembling the material for this work. I am obliged to the Labour Party staff, especially to G. R. Shepherd, H. S. Lindsay, W. W. Henderson, G. Grant McKenzie, and A. Luckhurst Scott. Parliamentary Party leaders to whom I am indebted include C. R. Attlee, George Lansbury, Hugh Dalton, Sir Stafford Cripps, and others. In the field of local government, I wish to acknowledge the aid of I. G. Gibbon, P. J. Dollan, Edward Cruse, George Archibald, and D. H. Daines. Among local Labour Party officials, H. Weate, J. P. Connolly, and H. E. Rogers were most helpful. A. E. Waterson, N. Smith, W. H. Green, and W. Harnwell assisted with information on Co-operative political activities.

To Fenner Brockway, Dr C. K. Cullen, Malcolm MacDonald, and Richard Law I owe thanks for explaining the position of various groups opposing Labour. Sir Walter Citrine kindly supplied data on the political interests of the Trade Unions. In the British academic world, I am grateful for the advice of Herman Finer, Harold J. Laski, E. F. M. Durbin, and

Hugh Gaitskell. Professors Samuel C. May of the University of California and Marshall E. Dimock of the University of Chicago provided valuable suggestions and introductions. I am especially indebted to Professors P. Orman Ray and J. C. Aikin of the University of California, who guided this study from its inception. My wife, Jane Snyder McHenry, has been my partner in every phase of the collection of materials and the writing, but she declines to be listed in her rightful place as co-author.

DEAN E. MCHENRY.

State College,
    Pennsylvania.
       January 1st, 1938.

THE LABOUR PARTY
IN TRANSITION
1931—1938

PART I
INTRODUCTION

THE RISE OF THE LABOUR PARTY

THE enfranchisement of town labourers by the Reform Act of 1867 gave rise to two parallel lines of British working class political activity which were later to converge to form the Labour Party. On one hand, the Trade Unions began seeking legislative concessions and direct representation in Parliament within the framework of the old Parties. On the other, Socialist societies were organized to urge the necessity for fundamental changes and for a workers' political party. The former possessed large membership and funds ; the latter offered direction and enthusiasm.

A. EARLY POLITICAL ACTIVITIES OF THE TRADE UNIONS

The Trade Unions of skilled artisans, which united in 1868 to form the loose confederation known as the Trades Union Congress, entered political activity in two ways : first, the Parliamentary Committee, established by the Congress of 1869, was charged with the responsibility of watching legislation, drafting parliamentary bills, interviewing Ministers, and representing the organized Unions between Congresses ; secondly, this lobbying activity was supplemented by participation in schemes for the election of working men to the House of Commons.

Individual Trade Unions were moderately successful in securing the election of their leaders to the House. In 1874, two working men candidates won seats ; in 1880, three ; in 1885, eleven ; in 1886, nine ; in 1892, fifteen ; in 1895, twelve.[1] Nearly all were elected as candidates of the Liberal Party ; local Liberal organizations often abstained from proposing opponents and endorsed the Labour representatives. Under Gladstone's leadership the relations of Liberals with the Trade Union representatives were very friendly.

Beginning in 1880 a new spirit of militancy was added to Trade Unionism by the advent of Unions of unskilled workers, which, unlike the more exclusive skilled craft Unions, required low contributions and paid only limited benefits. Dockers, gas workers, and general labourers were organized into large Unions. A series of successful strikes in the eighties and nineties was a great spur to the " New Unionism ". The aggressiveness of the new Unions permeated the old, and there was a general increase in membership and in the demand for the enactment of social legislation.

B. THE THREE MAJOR SOCIALIST SOCIETIES

While Trade Unionism was undergoing this transformation, three important Socialist societies—the Social Democratic Federation, the Fabian Society, and the Independent Labour Party—were formed.[2] Although they endorsed different policies and tactics, the three were agreed on the necessity of converting the Trade Union Movement to independent political action. Each in its own way worked toward that end.

The Democratic Federation was founded in 1881, and three years later took the name Social Democratic Federation.[3] Its original programme was reformist in character, but was soon changed to broad demands for socialization. The Federation's dominant leader, Henry Hyndman, was a revolutionary socialist, and successfully urged Marxist doctrines upon the organization. Although torn by dissensions and weakened by divisions, the S.D.F. had an important influence on the leaders of the " New Unionism " who passed through its ranks.[4]

The Fabian Society grew out of a small ethical society, " The Fellowship of the New Life ", which was founded in 1883 " for the purpose of reconstructing Society in accordance with the highest moral possibilities ".[5] Within a year, leaders of the group arrived by reason to the conviction that reconstruction of the economic system was necessary. A group of distinguished intellectuals who dominated the Society— Sidney and Beatrice Webb, Graham Wallas, Bernard Shaw, and others—proceeded to formulate and state the evolutionary socialist doctrine which later was accepted by the Labour Party. Rejecting orthodox Marxism the Fabians projected a moderate and practical programme of piecemeal nationalization and municipalization. Although never having a membership of more than three thousand, the Fabian Society, chiefly through its voluminous output of persuasive books and pamphlets, exerted a great influence over the political thought of the Labour Movement.

The Independent Labour Party, founded by Keir

Hardie in 1893, occupied a middle ground between revolutionist and evolutionist socialist thought. Its programme consisted largely of immediate reforms, but its ultimate object was " to secure the collective ownership of all the means of production, distribution and exchange ".[6] By its opportunist programme and aggressive tactics, the Independent Labour Party gathered into its ranks active young men, many of whom were Trade Union leaders.

Separately these Socialist societies worked for independent labour representation in Parliament. In this they were aided by two factors : the Trade Unions were growing impatient over the failure of the Liberals to keep pace in social legislation with changing industrial conditions ;[7] and an aroused class consciousness became especially manifest after the rise of the " New Unionism ".   During the nineties, Keir Hardie and the other socialists who urged labour representation in Parliament, obtained one concession after another from the Trades Union Congress.   By the turn of the century the Trade Unions were ready for joint political action with the Socialists.

C. THE LABOUR REPRESENTATION COMMITTEE

The Trades Union Congress of 1899, at which 1,200,000 organized workers were represented, adopted the following resolution which led to the formation of the Labour Party :[8]

That this Congress, having regard to its decisions in former years, and with a view of securing better representation of the interests of Labour in the House of Commons, hereby instructs the Parliamentary Committee to invite the co-operation of all co-operative, Socialistic, trade unions, and other working organizations to jointly co-operate on lines mutually agreed upon, in convening a Special Congress of representatives from such of the above-named organizations as may be willing to take part to devise ways and means for securing the return of an increased number of Labour members to the next Parliament.

The Joint Committee which was set up to plan the Conference implied in the foregoing resolution consisted of representatives of the Congress, the Independent Labour Party, the Social Democratic Federation, and the Fabian Society.

When the Conference met in February 1900, it accepted the Committee's draft plan for a " Federal Alliance " of Trade Unions, Trades Councils, Co-operatives, and Socialist societies.9 About half a million Trade Unionists and 70,000 members of Socialist and other societies were represented by the 129 Conference delegates. The Co-operatives, however, sent no delegates.

The Conference established the Labour Representation Committee, consisting of seven Trade Unionists, two members of the Independent Labour Party, two of the Social Democratic Federation, and one Fabian. It was agreed that the sole task of the Committee was to secure the election of workers' representatives to Parliament ; no common statement of policy was agreed upon. Ramsay MacDonald was elected Secretary of the Committee.

The Labour Representation Committee's first two years were difficult. During the first year it was forced to fight the " khaki " Election of 1900 without central funds and adequate preliminary organization. Two of the fifteen candidates advanced by the Committee were successful. Not only the Co-operatives failed to join in the united political effort, but the mineworkers chose to remain outside, and the Social Democratic Federation withdrew after the first year. In 1900-1 the Committee's total affiliated membership was only 375,000.

The tide began to turn in 1902, when, in the Taff Vale case, the House of Lords sustained an appellate court decision that a Trade Union's corporate funds were liable for tortious acts committed by its officials or members. By rendering Trade Union funds liable to damage suits, this decision placed a serious handicap on future use of the strike. Seeking by legislation to overcome the effect of the court ruling, the Unions advanced further into political action ; their instrument was the Labour Representation Committee.

In 1903 the Labour Representation Committee Conference agreed to voluntary political contributions of a penny a year for each member of affiliated organizations.[10] The following year this contribution was made compulsory. The independence of the Committee from the Trades Union Congress was recognized in 1904, when a resolution concerning the Committee was ruled out of order by the Congress Chairman.[11] The final attempt by opponents of joint political action to exclude Socialists from the Labour Representation Committee and place it solely on a Trade Union basis was defeated in 1905.[12] Between 1900 and 1906 three by-elections were won by Labour candidates ; during the same period the aggregate membership of organizations affiliated to the Labour Representation Committee was trebled.

D. Liberal-Labour Collaboration

During 1906, the Labour Representation Committee formally changed its name to Labour Party. It contested the General Election of that year in virtual alliance with the Liberals, and secured twenty-nine seats in the House of Commons. The Labour group in Parliament organized itself into the Parliamentary Labour Party. The Party's major legislative achievement of the period was its successful advocacy of a bill which nullified the ruling in the Taff Vale case by providing that the courts could not entertain a suit for damages against a Trade Union in its corporate capacity.

From 1906 to 1910, a period rich in social reforms, the Labour Party co-operated with the Liberal Government. In 1909 the mineworkers finally severed their connections with the Liberals and joined the Labour Party. Both of the Elections of 1910 were fought in virtual alliance with the Liberals ; in the January Election, Labour won forty seats; in December forty-two. After the Elections of 1910, when the Liberals lost seats, the Labour Members sat on the Government side.

In another judicial decision, affirmed by the House of Lords in 1909, a severe blow was struck at the very basis of Labour Party finance. In the Osborne case it was decided that Trade Unions could not use for political activities funds obtained by compulsory levies upon their members.[13] Up to this time Members of the House of Commons had received no compensation ; it had been the practice of individual Unions which sponsored candidates, and also of the Labour Party, to pay Labour M.P.s a salary of £200 and to provide a portion of their Election expenses. Since 1903 the Party had exacted from its candidates a pledge of loyalty to the Constitution and decisions of the Party. The pledge was discontinued in 1911 because of criticisms arising from the Osborne case.

Injunctions were served on several Unions restraining them from making political expenditures ; the Labour Party fought the Elections of 1910 under poor financial conditions. The situation was eased to some extent by voluntary contributions of societies and individuals, and, after 1911, by the public payment of parliamentary salaries.

From 1910 until the World War, the Labour Party was in a difficult situation. It could not afford to withdraw support from the Liberal Government both because the Party had no funds for another Election and because precipitating a third Election in rapid succession would be unpopular politically. For some time the Liberals postponed action on legislation to remedy the situation resulting from the Osborne decision, but in 1913, the Labour Party finally succeeded in obtaining the enactment of a compromise measure. The Trades Union Act of 1913 authorized Trade Unions to collect and spend special funds for political purposes if a majority of the membership authorized such action, provided that the political fund was kept separate from other Union funds, and provided further that members who objected to the levy might give notice and be exempted.[14] The latter practice is known popularly as " contracting out ".

During the World War a division appeared in the ranks of the Labour Party. Arthur Henderson, G. N. Barnes and others represented the Party in the Coalition Government, and both the Party and the Trades Union Congress were committed to support the war. On the other hand, the Independent Labour Party, including Ramsay MacDonald and Philip Snowden, opposed the war and refused to participate in the Government.[15] Before the Armistice, however, a growing unrest appeared in the Labour Movement ; the Party began an examination of war aims ; the Trade Unions were involved increasingly in impromptu and unauthorized strikes ; international socialist connections were renewed.

A 1917 special Party Conference decided to send a delegation to a general International Socialist Congress at Stockholm. In the controversy over the British Government's refusal to issue passports to the delegates, Henderson resigned from the War Cabinet. An inter-allied Socialist Conference was held in London in August 1917.[16]

E. LABOUR'S RISE TO NATIONAL POWER

In 1918 the Labour Party first emerged as a major National Party. Local Labour Parties were re-organized; and persons now could join the Party directly as individual members, whereas previously, participation in Party work had been through membership in a local Trades Council, a nationally affiliated Trade Union or Socialist society. The year 1918 also is a landmark in the history of the Party because in that year a statement of aims was adopted which was, for the first time, definitely socialistic in character. This policy declaration included demands for a minimum standard of living, gradual socialization of the means of production, the capital levy and taxation on the basis of ability to pay, and use of surplus wealth for the common good. In the General Election of 1918 the Party proposed 361 candidates, of whom 57 were elected ; nearly two and one-quarter million votes were polled by it. Because the Asquith Liberals suffered heavy losses to both the Coalition and the Labourites, Labour became the chief Party of the Opposition ; but its three foremost leaders, Ramsay MacDonald, Arthur Henderson and Philip Snowden, were defeated.

During 1920 the growing militancy of the Trade Unions and the Labour Party was revealed in their plans for direct action to resist the proposed British intervention in Soviet Russia.[17] Further success was achieved in the General Election of 1922, when the Party secured the election of 142 of its 414 candidates. At the same time, the Liberals lost heavily to the

Labour Party, both in leadership and votes. Membership of the Party and of the Trade Unions increased rapidly ; the Party was aggressive in local politics and obtained a majority in a few municipalities ; further Parliamentary gains were recorded in the Election of 1923, in which Labour won 191 seats.

The 1923 Election gave no Party a Commons majority. Although the Conservatives won a plurality, their losses indicated popular rejection of their programme ; both Liberal and Labour were disinclined to enter a coalition. The only solution which appeared practicable was for Labour to accept office with Liberal support. Ramsay MacDonald in January 1924 formed the first Labour Government—recruiting a surprising array of talent and experience.

Labour's legislative achievements in office were modest : a liberalized housing subsidy act was passed ; grants for education and social services were increased. In foreign affairs, an agreement was reached with France on reparations and the Ruhr ; Britain recognized the Russian Soviet Government. Domestically, the Labour Government was not able to liquidate unemployment ; indeed it was embarrassed by serious strikes of railwaymen, dockers, and builders. Nine troubled months in office ended in October 1924. The incident over which the Government fell was its failure to prosecute an alleged Communist editor charged with sedition ; however, a break was the inevitable result of the lack of common aims on the part of the Liberal and Labour Parties.

During the Election campaign which followed there was a " Red " scare, aroused by a Foreign Office protest to the U.S.S.R. against alleged subversive propaganda in Great Britain. To substantiate the charge, the notorious "Zinovieff Letter" was produced ; it purported to be an instruction on tactics from the Communist International to the British Communist Party.[18] Although the authenticity of the letter has never been established, its effect upon the Election was apparent ; Labour lost forty-two seats, although it gained in popular vote ; the Liberals lost about three-fourths of their seats ; the large Conservative majority supported a new Government led by Mr Stanley Baldwin.

F. The General Strike and Its Aftermath

The next four years of Conservative Government were marked by militant industrial action on the part of the Trade Unions. In an effort to halt the gradual reduction of their living standards, coal miners in 1926 refused to accept wage cuts and longer hours. On April 30th mineworkers were locked out ; on May 4th a sympathetic " General Strike " began.[19] Only the " first line " of workers was called out—transport workers and railwaymen, iron and steel workers, builders and printers. The strikers were orderly, but resolute. The Government vigorously opposed the strike, and arrested and imprisoned many.

When the mineworkers refused to accept a compromise proposal, the Trades Union Congress called off the sympathetic strike eight days after the walk-out.

Although the miners continued for six months to resist the proposed wage cuts and increased hours, they eventually were forced to return to work under the owners' terms.

The Conservative Government's reprisal came in the Trades Disputes and Trades Union Act of 1927, which curbed sympathetic strikes, placed restrictions on picketing, and forbade the affiliation of State employees with non-State workers.[20]   Most serious to the Labour Party was the provision that a Trade Union might not collect a political levy except from those members who express in writing their desire to contribute.   In popular terms, " contracting in " was substituted for " contracting out ".   The effect of this provision was damaging to the Labour Party ; between 1927 and 1928 the Party lost more than a million Trade Unionist members ; its finances have never fully recovered.

G. THE SECOND LABOUR GOVERNMENT

Aided by a deepening trade depression, the Labour Party made a strong appeal at the 1929 Election, won 288 seats, and polled a popular vote of more than eight million.   Although it had the largest number of Members in the House of Commons, the Party lacked a majority, and the second Labour Government, like the first, was dependent upon Liberal support. Precluded from advancing sweeping socialistic measures the Government occupied itself with preparations for the Disarmament Conference, with a public works programme, and with reforms in housing, education, and transport.

Tossed about on the troubled waters of the world economic chaos, the Labour Government muddled along, satisfying neither its Socialist supporters nor its external critics.   Eventually it was faced in July 1931 with the recommendation of the Expert's Commission headed by Sir George May that governmental expenditures be reduced by £96,000,000 ; two-thirds of this was to come from unemployment benefits, and the rest chiefly from cuts in the pay of civil servants and teachers, and reductions in social service activities.

During July and August the drain on British gold reserves reached serious proportions.   American and French bankers allegedly laid down as conditions for a projected loan that the Government budget be balanced and that economies be effected.   A majority of the Cabinet supported the Trades Union Congress position that the proposal for the reduction of unemployment benefits must be rejected.   Sidney Webb reported that Mr MacDonald was empowered on Sunday, August 23rd, to present his resignation to the King.[21] It was assumed that Mr Baldwin would be called to form a Conservative Government.

H.   FORMATION OF THE " NATIONAL " GOVERNMENT

But, instead, the King commissioned Mr MacDonald to form a " National " Government containing representatives of the three major political Parties.   Philip Snowden, J. H. Thomas, Lord Sankey, and a few minor Labour leaders accepted posts in the new Government.   Liberal and Conservative participation in the Coalition Government was approved officially by their respective Party meetings. The Parliamentary Labour Party, however, indicated its disapproval of Labourite participation in the National Government by removing MacDonald from Party Leadership and electing Arthur Henderson. Subsequently, all Labour supporters of the Government were expelled from the Party by the National Executive Committee on the grounds that their action was incompatible with Party membership. All local Labour Parties remained loyal to the official Party organization.

Professor Harold J. Laski has termed the events leading to the formation of the National Government a " Palace Revolution ", and has shown convincingly that the King acted arbitrarily in recognizing MacDonald, no longer a Party leader, as Prime Minister of the Coalition.[22] The new Government made reductions in expenditures, but was forced to abandon the gold standard. Shortly thereafter the Government ordered a dissolution and set an Election date.

The National Government asked the electorate for a " doctor's mandate " to deal with the problems of the crisis. It was a bitter and frantic campaign. The Coalition spokesmen convinced a great majority of the voters that the Labour Party stood for what one of their outstanding ex-leaders (Snowden) called " Bolshevism run mad ". The pound, financial institutions, even Post Office savings allegedly would be endangered by a Socialist Government.[23] The victory of the Government was overwhelming ; supporters of the Coalition won ninety-one per cent. of the seats contested and two-thirds of the popular vote. With only forty-six seats remaining, the Parliamentary Labour Party was reduced to its pre-war strength.

Created by the fusion of the political efforts of the Trade Unions and Socialist societies, the Labour Party had welded effectively the contributions of the two chief elements in the " Federal Alliance ". The Trade Unions had furnished the bulk of membership and financial strength, stability and solidarity. The Socialist societies had provided ideology, leadership, and ardour. The combination had been an effective one ; it had been so powerful that the Party had gained popular strength steadily in overcoming adverse court decisions and legislation, internal controversies, and lack of funds.

But in 1931 the Party lost its outstanding leaders ; its parliamentary representation was reduced to an insignificant size ; its future was uncertain.

CHAPTER ONE

REFERENCES

[1] A. W. Humphrey, *A History of Labour Representation* (London, 1912), Appendix.

[2] General works covering the early British Socialist Movement include : Joseph Clayton, *The Rise and Decline of Socialism in Great Britain, 1884-1924* (London, 1926) ; Max Beer, *A History of British Socialism* (London, 1929) ; Godfrey Elton, *England Arise ! A Study of the Pioneering Days of the Labour Movement* (London, 1931) ; B. C. De Montgomery, *British and Continental Labour Policy* (London, 1922) ; G. D. H. Cole, *A Short History of the British Working Class Movement, 1789-1927* (London, 1932).

[3] The story of the Social Democratic Federation is told in : Frederick J. Gould, *Hyndman, Prophet of Socialism* (London, 1928) ; Henry Hyndman, *Record of an Adventurous Life* (London, 1911) ; H. W. Lee and E. Archbold, *Social Democracy in Britain, Fifty Years of the Socialist Movement* (London, 1935).

[4] William Morris, Eleanor Marx (youngest daughter of Karl Marx), and others withdrew in 1884 and formed the Socialist League. The S.D.F. joined the Labour Party in 1900 and left it in 1901. Some of the Federation's branches broke away in 1905 and 1908. In 1911 it merged into the British Socialist Party. During the war that organization split. Hyndman and a minority supported the war. In 1920 Hyndman's group reverted to the old name of Social Democratic Federation and rejoined the Labour Party. The British Socialist Party became the basis of the Communist Party.

[5] Edward R. Pease, *The History of the Fabian Society* (London, 1925), p. 235.

6 *The Independent Labour Party Report of the First General Conference* (Glasgow, 1893), p. 4 ; William Stewart, *J. Keir Hardie* (London, 1925).

7 R. H. Tawney, *The British Labour Movement* (New Haven, 1925), pp. 22-4.

8 W. J. Davis, *The British Trades Union Congress, History and Recollections*, Vol. ii (London, 1916), p. 170.

9 *Report of the Conference on Labour Representation held in Memorial Hall, London, on Tuesday, 27th February, 1900*, etc., pp. 8-18.

10 *Report of the Third Annual Conference of the Labour Representation Committee, 1903* (London, 1903), pp. 33-6.

11 Humphrey, op. cit., p. 161.

12 *Report of the Fifth Annual Conference of the Labour Representation Committee, 1905* (London, 1905), pp. 45-6.

13 Amalgamated Society of Railway Servants *v.* Osborne, House of Lords, England (1910).

14 2 and 3 George V, Chapter 30.

15 Philip Viscount Snowden, *An Autobiography* (London, 1934), Vol. i, pp. 349-520 ; H. Hessell Tiltman, *James Ramsay MacDonald, Labour's Man of Destiny* (London, 1930), pp. 57-70.

16 *Report of the Seventeenth Annual Conference of the Labour Party, 1918* (London, 1918), pp. 4-8. Hereafter Labour Party Conference reports are cited : *1918 Conference, 1919 Conference, 1920 Conference*, etc.

17 William P. Maddox, *Foreign Relations in British Labour Politics* (Cambridge, Mass., 1934), pp. 190-5.

18 Cole, op. cit., Vol. iii, pp. 194-5.

19 Documents concerning the strike have been collected and published by the Trades Union Congress in *The Mining Crisis and the National Strike, 1926, Official Reports* (London, 1927).

[20] 17 and 18 George V, Chapter 22.

[21] Sidney Webb, *What Happened in 1931 : A Record*, Fabian Tract No. 237 (1932), p. 8.

[22] Harold J. Laski, *The Crisis and the Constitution : 1931 and After* (London, 1932), p. 34. A different point of view is expressed in Ian Colvin, " A Royal Week End ", *Atlantic Monthly*, Vol. cxlix (April 1932), pp. 501-8.

[23] Arthur W. MacMahon, " The British General Election of 1931," *American Political Science Review*, Vol. xxvi (April 1932), pp. 333-45.

PART II

THE PARTY MACHINE

Chapter Two

THE NATIONAL PARTY ORGANIZATION

A. Structure of the Labour Party

The Labour Party still retains the essential features of the original " Federal Alliance " of working class organizations, united for political action. The Trade Unions continue to contribute the bulk of membership and funds, holding, thereby, the ultimate control over both organization and policy. Socialist societies furnish much leadership and make important contributions to policy, but remain numerically small. One large Co-operative society has affiliated nationally with the Labour Party, and has increased materially the Party's local strength in the London region.

The greatest structural change, however, was the Party's constitutional modification of 1918, under which individual members have been accepted into local Labour Parties, and the local Parties have been developed within the national organization. These local agencies have taken over a major portion of the Party's financial and organizational responsibilities in the constituencies. Ward, Constituency, and Borough Parties carry on the basic work of the Labour Party, both in " quiet " periods and in preparation for municipal and General Elections.

For the year 1936, the Labour Party had a total paid-up affiliated membership of 2,444,357, of which

seventy-three Trade Unions accounted for 1,968,538 ;
eight Socialist societies had 9,125 members ; the Royal
Arsenal Co-operative Society paid fees for 36,000 of
its vast membership ; and local Parties reported
430,694.

The various affiliated organizations are represented
at the Annual Conference of the Labour Party in
proportion to the size of their membership. The
Conference elects a National Executive Committee, a
Secretary, and a Treasurer. The Executive Committee
is responsible for the Central Office and the supervision
of the Party organization generally. The local
branches of the Labour Party are semi-autonomous,
but increasingly are subjected to national controls.
The Labour Members of Parliament constitute the
Parliamentary Labour Party which, though dependent
on the Party organization at Election time, afterward
becomes quite independent except for such restrictions
as it may choose to accept. It also performs the
important function of selecting the Party's Leader.
The National Council of Labour—a joint committee
composed of representatives from the Trades Union
Congress General Council, the Labour Party Executive,
and the Parliamentary Party Executive Committee—
discusses questions affecting the Labour Movement as
a whole and attempts to agree on a common policy.

B. Composition and Procedure of the Annual Conference

The Annual Conference is the highest authority of
the Labour Party ; theoretically it decides Party policy

and exercises general control over the Party organization. Actually, however, owing to the nature of its composition, it is largely restricted to the ratification of resolutions prepared or approved by the Party's Executive. The Conference is made up of delegates from affiliated bodies, and three types of *ex officio* delegates, namely, members of the National Executive Committee, Labour Members of Parliament, and endorsed parliamentary candidates. Affiliated Trade Unions are allocated one delegate for each 5,000 members or fraction thereof; Constituency Parties have the same representation, but each may send an additional woman delegate if the combined individual and women's membership is over 2,500. Central Parties and Trades Councils in Boroughs with more than one constituency, and Federations of Constituency Parties are allowed one delegate each.

The right to vote in the Conference is accorded on the basis of affiliated membership. One voting card is issued to each affiliated organization for each 1,000 members or part thereof. The Conferences of recent years have ranged in size between 600 and 750 delegates and generally have met for five days.

For many years the Conference has been held between the last Monday in September and the second Monday in October. This season has proven rather unsatisfactory both because it interferes with municipal campaigning, and because it follows so closely the Annual Meeting of the Trades Union Congress, which is devoting itself increasingly to political matters.

These considerations and others led the Conference of
1937 to change the meeting time to Whitsuntide. The
problem of whether the next Conference will come at
Whitsuntide 1938 or 1939 was not settled, but left to
the Executive. The choice of meeting place of each
Conference usually is delegated to the Executive
Committee. The policy has been to alternate the
Conferences between the larger municipalities of the
country.

Arrangements for each Conference are made by a
committee elected by the previous Conference. This
committee plans the order of the agenda, determines
time limits on debate, appoints tellers, and approves
the introduction of emergency resolutions. The names
and addresses of delegates must be filed with the Party
Secretary in advance. Affiliated organizations may
submit two resolutions each, which are issued in a
First Agenda. The same limit applies to amendments
to resolutions in the *First Agenda*, which together with
nominations for elective officers, must be submitted
for the *Final Agenda* two or three months before the
convening. The Conference can consider no business
except that on the *Agenda*, unless the Executive or
Arrangements Committee so recommends ; nor can
it entertain a resolution on any point on which it has
made a declaration of policy during the last three
years, unless the Executive deems it of " immediate
importance ". These restrictions were initiated to
reduce the volume of Conference business and to ensure
time for preliminary discussion of matters to be
considered.

A number of qualifications must be met by delegates : all delegates must accept and conform to the constitution and policy of the Party ; they must be members or officials of the organization appointing them ; if Trade Unionists, they must have paid the political levy ; if Members of Parliament, they must be in the Parliamentary Labour Party. Candidates who oppose Labour, their supporters, and members of Parties or organizations ineligible to affiliate with the Party may not serve as delegates to the Conference. The Communist Party, the British Union of Fascists, and several allegedly ancillary organizations have been thus " black listed ". Representatives from Constituency and Federations of Constituency Parties must be voters in the area, unless they are Members of Parliament or candidates.

C. DOMINANT FORCES IN THE ANNUAL CONFERENCE

The annual report of the National Executive Committee to the Conference is chiefly a record of events and accomplishments. In addition, the Executive submits draft statements of policy to the Conference for review. Unless Executive reports are challenged successfully by the Conference, they are deemed approved. The business of the Conference increasingly is limited to the proposals of the Executive, and the support of the Executive is nearly indispensable to the passage of a resolution.

In the six Conferences, 1932-7, the Executive was defeated only ten times. In only five of these instances had the matter rejected been proposed by the

Executive ; all other resolutions originating in the Executive were passed by the Conference or withdrawn. There were three defeats in 1932, four in 1933, one in 1934, one in 1935, and one in 1936. Of these, the most important matters passed over the Executive opposition were as follows : a resolution for the nationalization of joint-stock banks ; a resolution requiring the next Labour Government to introduce and stand or fall on definite Socialist legislation ; and a resolution for workers' participation in the management of socialized industries.

The ability of the Executive to secure the adoption of its own resolutions is due to the fact that the large Trade Union vote nearly always unites in its support. At recent Conferences, delegates from the five largest Trade Unions have held a clear majority of the total votes. The five Unions and their memberships affiliated to the Labour Party in 1937 were :

Trade Union	Affiliated Membership
Mineworkers' Federation	400,000
Transport and General Workers	301,000
General and Municipal Workers	242,000
National Union of Railwaymen	214,919
United Textile Factory Workers	130,507

The record of all Unions large and small, in getting their resolutions and motions accepted is striking ; about one-third of Trade Union proposals reach the Conference floor, and nearly all are adopted. Defeats of propositions sponsored by the larger industrial bodies are rare indeed.

The fact that Trade Unions directly propose few matters to the Conference is due in part to the satisfaction of most Unions with the work of the Executive and, perhaps, to the dearth of interest in Party affairs on the industrial side of the Labour Movement. The Executive rarely opposes resolutions and amendments submitted by the Trade Unions and almost never does it stand against a large Union. This is doubtless due to the preponderant voting strength of the Unions and to the fact that the Trade Unions have had a majority on the Party Executive.

D. RANK AND FILE PARTICIPATION IN CONFERENCE WORK

Local Labour Parties present the bulk of resolutions, motions, and amendments to the Conference, constituting eighty-five to ninety-five per cent. of the total on the *Final Agenda* between 1932 and 1937. Around ten per cent. of these reaches the floor of the Conference, and about three per cent. is passed.

The reason for the large number of matters raised by local Parties is not difficult to find : the local Labour Parties have lacked an adequate central organization or conference through which they may co-ordinate their policy ; their delegates are sent to the Conference with a great variety of instructions. The result is that local Parties have difficulty in uniting on an issue, while the Trade Unions, because of their large blocks of votes and the fact that their attitudes have been crystallized at the Trades Union Congress a month previously, appear even more powerful than their great voting strength would ensure.

In recent years, the machinery of the Federations of Constituency Parties, of the unofficial National Association of Constituency Parties, and the device of composite resolutions have reduced the number of outright Conference defeats of local Parties.

Socialist societies affiliated to the Party submit a very small number of resolutions to the Conference and have fair success in securing their adoption.

Inasmuch as the *Agenda* has grown to formidable length, it is necessary to use every available means to reduce the amount of business with which the Conference must deal. The *Final Agenda* for the last six Conferences averaged about 350 resolutions, amendments, and amendments to amendments. A relatively small proportion of these reached the discussion stage of a Conference. Some are excluded by the three year rule ; others are withdrawn in favour of similar resolutions ; many are not moved, or are withdrawn at the request or suggestion of the Executive ; some are referred to the Executive ; a number are not reached in the time allocated to the general subject ; a few allegedly disappear without any reason being given ; in preliminary discussions of delegates from proposing organizations, some are combined into a few composite resolutions. At the 1933 Conference seventeen composite resolutions were agreed to in discussions on the eve of the Conference and presented to the Conference in printed form. There were nine composite resolutions in 1935.

E. Evaluation of the Annual Conference

The Arrangements Committee for the 1933 Conference submitted a memorandum urging that the fourfold purpose of the Annual Conference was : (1) to consider the annual report of the Executive ; (2) to review and formulate policy on guidance of the Executive ; (3) to give the rank and file a chance to initiate policy ; (4) to " educate " the Movement.

In practice not all within these limits can be accomplished. The report of the Executive forms the basis for much of the Conference business. Executive policy reports and resolutions constitute a large part of the remainder. The rank and file of Party workers who are in the local Parties, have a rather small chance to initiate policy. In 1932, when the revolt against " gradualism " was strongest, local Parties, with Trade Union support, forced through the Conference over Executive opposition, two important policy resolutions. But since 1932 local Parties have played a role of urging the Trade Unions "left", but have enjoyed little success.

On the face of it, the plan of allowing one Conference vote for each 1,000 members of affiliated national organizations and Constituency Parties would appear in keeping with the Party's democratic tradition. The members of the different kinds of affiliated organizations, however, make widely varied contributions to the Party. Many Trade Unionists contract in and have their fourpence halfpenny per year sent to Transport House, but do little else for the Party. On the other hand, many local Party members devote

3

large amounts of time and energy to active Party work in the constituencies. Few Trade Unions have devised any democratic machinery for the discussion of issues brought up on Conference Agendas, and many leave important decisions to an executive committee of paid officials or to a single dominant leader. Constituency Parties commonly hold general meetings for intensive discussions of Conference Agendas.

A serious problem arises from the fact that many local Labour Parties are unable to send delegates to the Conferences. The greatest barrier is financial ; few Parties have funds available to pay the expenses of their representatives. In addition, in some Parties it is difficult to find competent delegates who are able to leave their jobs over the Conference period. The Executive proposed a constitutional amendment in 1937 to permit proxy representation of Constituency Parties by Federations or Central Parties. The Executive dropped the proposition before the vote was taken, and it was defeated. Certainly there are many valid arguments against allowing proxy voting, but some solution—perhaps the pooling of expenses among all affiliated organizations—is needed.

A certain unwieldiness of the Conference arises from the fact that this body of 600 to 750 meets for only five days once yearly to review the affairs of a great political Party. It is precluded from discussing at length more than a half-dozen issues of importance, and its decisions on these may generally be predicted with accuracy because of the cohesiveness of the big Trade Union delegates that support the recommendations of the

Executive. The Labour Party Conference does not represent perfectly the diverse elements within the Party, but it is far superior to American Party Conventions in atmosphere and achievement.

The value of the Conference is not confined to the formal discussions and sessions, for it is important, too, that it brings together into a fellowship representatives of the scattered groups which form the " Federal Alliance ". The unity of the Movement is re-emphasized, and the delegates take back to their organizations something of the spirit of the Party as a whole. It is regrettable that some sections of the Party are precluded from sending delegates.

F. The National Executive Committee

The National Executive Committee, generally referred to as the Executive, is the *ad interim* body which directs the Party organization between Conferences, and exerts an influence which is decisive in nearly every issue before the Conference. The Executive, since 1937, is composed of twenty-five committee-men and a Treasurer, all elected by the Conference. For purposes of nomination and election to the Executive, affiliated organizations are divided into four groups : the Trade Unions nominate and elect twelve committee-men ; Socialist, Co-operative, and Professional societies choose one ; local Parties, seven ; and all affiliates participate in nominating and electing five women members.

Before the 1937 changes, nominations for each group were submitted to the whole Conference by organizations within the groups. All organizations voted for candidates in each division, a procedure which placed the ultimate choice of the whole Executive in the hands of the big Trade Unions. In a second reform, the elective membership of the Executive was increased from twenty-three to twenty-five, by adding two representatives of local Parties.

Consultations held by the Executive during 1936-7 in various parts of the country disclosed widespread dissatisfaction in the local Parties over their lack of influence in national Party matters. A " sense of constraint " and " frustration " adversely affected morale. Individual membership had increased greatly in recent years, but additional representation on Executive had not been granted. Executive members with an understanding of problems in the Constituencies were urgently needed. In the voting on the proposition for increase of the Executive size, the Trade Union delegates divided about evenly and the majority in favour of the change was 274,000. Over a million majority carried the proposal for direct election for representatives by the various groups. The majority for putting the new plan into effect at once was overwhelming.

The powers of the Executive are very great : (1) its interpretation of the Party Constitution, Standing Orders, and Rules is final, and it may enforce them by any necessary action, including discharging organizations and expelling individuals ; (2) it may confer with the Parliamentary Labour Party on the work or programme of the Party ; (3) it may propose to the

Conference policy or other resolutions, or amendments to the Constitution or Standing Orders ; (4) it makes the final endorsement of parliamentary candidates ; (5) it has power to adjudicate disputes between affiliated organizations ; (6) it supervises the day to day conduct of the Party machinery through the Head Office ; (7) it places before the Conference a report of the year's work, and makes recommendations on matters of organization and policy.

In addition, there are a number of other powers and duties with which the Executive is charged. It arranges the representation of the Party in the Labour and Socialist International, in the National Council of Labour, on Joint Committees with the Trades Union Congress General Council, and maintains a sub-committee on relations with the Co-operative Party. At Election times, the Executive joins the Executive Committee of the Parliamentary Party in issuing a manifesto stating Party aims and programme. Its sub-committees on organization, finance and general purposes, research and publicity, and elections keep in touch with and advise the permanent staff of the Party ; the sub-committees on policy and international affairs frame memoranda and programme both for immediate public statements and for submission to the Conference.

A remarkable continuity exists in the personnel of the Executive. In the seven years since the 1931 Conference, thirteen of the regular elective members of the Executive have served for the full period, and three for six years. This tendency to re-elect members of the Executive has resulted in the maintenance of a preponderant majority of experienced committee-men, making possible a continuity of policy, but with the obvious hazard of stagnation.

ELECTIVE PERSONNEL OF THE EXECUTIVE, 1931-7

	1931-1932	1932-1933	1933-1934	1934-1935	1935-1936	1936-1937	1937-1938
I.—Trade Union Section :							
Hirst, Transport Workers	*	*	*	*	*	*	*
Clynes, General and Municipal	*	*	*	*	*	*	*
Roberts, Typographical	*	*	*	*	*	*	*
Brothers, Textile	*	*	*	*	*	*	*
Swan, Mineworkers	*	*	*	*	*	*	*
Robinson, Distributive	*	*	*	*	*	*	*
Kaylor, Engineering	*	*	*	*	*	*	*
Walker, Iron and Steel	—	*	*	*	*	*	*
Compton, Vehicle Builders	*	*	*	*	*	*	—
Lathan, Railway Clerks	*	*	*	*	*	—	—
Smith, Boot and Shoe	*	*	*	*	—	—	—
Henderson, Railwaymen	—	—	—	—	*	*	*
Dobbie, Railwaymen	—	*	*	*	—	—	—
Dobbs, Boot and Shoe	—	—	—	—	—	*	*
Ridley, Railway Clerks	—	—	—	—	—	*	*
Prain, Electrical	—	—	—	—	—	—	*
Dennison, Iron and Steel	*	—	—	—	—	—	—
Turner, Textiles	*	—	—	—	—	—	—
Gooch, Agricultural	—	—	—	—	*	—	—
II.—Socialist and Co-operative Section :							
Williams, Royal Arsenal	*	*	*	*	—	—	—
Green, Royal Arsenal	—	—	—	—	*	*	*
III.—Constituency Organizations' Section :							
Dallas, Local Party	*	*	*	*	*	*	*
Dalton, Local Party	*	*	*	*	*	*	*
Morrison, Local Party	*	*	*	*	*	*	*
Toole, Local Party	—	*	*	—	*	*	—
Jenkins, Local Party	*	—	—	—	*	*	—
Lansbury, Local Party	*	*	—	—	—	—	—
Cripps, Local Party	—	—	—	*	—	—	*
Attlee, Local Party	—	—	—	*	—	—	—
Trevelyan, Local Party	—	—	*	—	—	—	—
Laski, Local Party	—	—	—	—	—	—	*
Pritt, Local Party	—	—	—	—	—	—	*
Noel-Baker, Local Party	—	—	—	—	—	—	*

	1931-1932	1932-1933	1933-1934	1934-1935	1935-1936	1936-1937	1937-1938
IV.—*Women Members :*							
Gould, Local Party	*	*	*	*	*	*	*
Lawrence, Fabian Society	*	*	*	*	*	*	*
Adamson, Local Party	*	*	*	*	*	*	*
Carlin, Transport Workers	*	*	*	*	*	*	—
Smith, Local Party	—	*	*	*	—	—	—
Dollan, Scottish Socialist	—	—	—	—	*	*	*
Wilkinson, Local Party	—	—	—	—	—	—	*
Manning, Labour Teachers	*	—	—	—	—	—	—

The Executive meets regularly about once a month. The Leader of the Parliamentary Labour Party is an *ex officio* member. The possibility of having an inter-locking directorate with the same leaders managing both the political and industrial sides of the Movement is avoided by a Party rule that members of the Trades Union Congress General Council are ineligible to serve on the Executive.

The Executive selects its own Chairman, who acts also as Chairman of the Labour Party. Few Chairmen of recent years have been prominent national figures ; five were Trade Unionists, only one of whom could be considered a key figure on the industrial side of the Movement. Dr Dalton, 1936-7 Chairman, is a prominent parliamentary leader. Mr George Dallas, 1937-8 Chairman, has contributed to the Party's work in rural areas.

Fifteen of the twenty-three elective members of the 1935-6 Executive contested constituencies in the 1935 Election ; eleven were successful. Significantly, all the Trade Unionists who contested constituencies in 1935 won ; of the four members of the Executive who were defeated, two represented local Parties, and two represented women.

The 1937-8 Executive, the first chosen under the new plan, contains more distinguished figures than any one since the MacDonald defection. Including the Leader and Treasurer, thirteen are M.P.s, of whom six— Attlee, Clynes, Roberts, Dalton, Cripps, and Morrison —have served as Ministers or Junior Ministers in Labour Governments. Cripps and Pritt are talented barristers, Laski is one of the best known political scientists living. Robinson is Secretary of the important Distributive Workers' Union.

The Secretary of the Labour Party is elected by the Conference on recommendation of the Executive. Under the terms of a 1934 Conference decision, this officer must give full time to Party work and may not become a Member of Parliament. The Secretary is the managing director of the Labour Party ; he supervises the work of all departments and is responsible to the Executive for carrying out its decisions. This high office is of great importance. It has been held by only three men since 1900. Mr Ramsay MacDonald occupied it until 1911, when Arthur Henderson began his twenty-three year term which ended in 1934 with the appointment of his Assistant Secretary, J. S. Middleton, to succeed him.

Middleton was a printer by trade, but soon after his arrival in London from the provinces in 1902 he became part-time secretary to Mr MacDonald and the Labour Representation Committee. After more than thirty years of continuous service in the Party, he assumed the title of Secretary ; he had already borne a large share of the responsibility of the office throughout MacDonald's and Henderson's long careers in Parliament.

G. THE NATIONAL COUNCIL OF LABOUR

Since 1921, when the Labour Party and the Trades Union Congress made an agreement for active collaboration, there has been a joint policy committee containing representatives of the General Council of the Trades Union Congress, the Executive of the Labour Party, and the Executive Committee of the Parliamentary Labour Party. Until 1931, the three bodies were represented equally on the Committee, which was designated the National Joint Council. After the crisis of 1931, however, the Council was reconstituted to represent " more adequately " the industrial, political, and parliamentary sections of the Movement. In its revised form, the Council contains seven representatives of the Trade Unions and only three each of the Labour Party and the Parliamentary Party. Regular monthly meetings are held for the discussion of all questions affecting the Labour Movement as a whole, on which an attempt is made to form a common policy.

The new Council has been most active during the last four years, and an increasing number of questions are deemed of common interest. In 1932, the Council declared Labour's policy on the Sino-Japanese conflict ; in 1933, on the German dictatorship, the alleged miscarriage of justice in India, the imprisonment of

British radical leaders, broadcasting, the taxation of Co-operative societies, and the proposed embargo on Russian trade. The Council united with the Co-operative Union, the Federation of British Co-operative societies, in organizing a national demonstration on unemployment. Also in 1933, the Council announced its decision that it should be responsible for the selection of speakers whenever a section of the Movement is invited to use the broadcasting facilities.

The group in 1934 assumed the name National Council of Labour, but retained the same constitution with its Trade Union majority. After consultation with the Co-operative Party, the Council restated its position in opposition to a " united front " proposed by the Communist Party. A deputation from the Council presented to the Prime Minister a resolution urging Britain to take the lead in disarmament, and expressing a desire for the entry of the Soviet Union into the League of Nations. A joint anti-war and anti-fascism campaign was conducted by the Council. During 1935 the activities of the Council assumed even more importance, and policy declarations were issued on the Italo-Abyssinian dispute, unemployment assistance, Russian assassinations, workers' control in industry, and old age pensions. The Council also co-operated with the League of Nations Union in carrying out the " Peace Ballot " to provide the public with the means of expressing views on the vital questions concerning war and peace.

The Council in 1935 attempted to broaden its scope by inviting the National Co-operative Authority to become associated with it, but the Authority declined, stating that the Council was concerned with many things outside the official interests of the Co-operative Movement. The Co-operatives did participate, however, in a pro-sanctions joint demonstration in June 1936.

During 1936 Labour's policy toward the Spanish rebellion was framed at a special Conference called by the National Council of Labour ; the Council issued initial appeals for relief funds for use in Spain. The Council in 1937 mainly was occupied with the Spanish situation, co-ordinating the efforts of the three bodies, and co-operating with the Labour and Socialist International and the International Federation of Trade Unions. Labour's modest pension plan, widely publicized in the Immediate Programme, was drawn up and published by the National Council of Labour.

Although the acceptance of National Council decisions theoretically is voluntary on the part of the participating organizations, the structure of the Trade Union and Labour Movements and the publicity given to Council action makes rejection by the Labour Party or the Parliamentary Party virtually impossible. If, on a specific issue, the Labour parliamentary group declined to accept the National Council's stand, Labour's opponents would gain support for the frequent charge that the forces of Labour are divided. Similarly, considerable embarrassment would result if the Party Conference or Executive refused to accept as final a Council decision. To maintain the front of internal harmony, declarations of the National Council of Labour must be followed.

THE CENTRAL OFFICE : FINANCIAL AND ORGANIZATIONAL PROBLEMS

A. NATIONAL AND LOCAL PARTY FINANCE

MANY of the Labour Party's pressing problems remain unsolved because of the lack of adequate funds. Opposed by the Conservatives, whose money-raising powers are very great, and the Liberals, who still have access to considerable reserves, this Party which has been built on the pennies of the working class has been confronted with an almost overwhelming obstacle to success. Its achievements at the polls have been due to the devotion of large numbers of people to the Labour cause and their willingness to give their time and energies to the essential work of canvassing and organizing. Under the Party's ingenious system of finance, many people give small amounts, instead of the usual method of political financing whereby a few make large contributions.

The basis of Labour Party financing is the affiliation fee. At the present time, the national Party's funds are raised by the payment of fourpence halfpenny per member per year by each allied Trade Union, Cooperative society, Socialist organization, and Constituency Labour Party. Central Parties in the larger municipalities contribute uniform affiliation

fees of four pounds ten shillings per year. Affiliation
fees amount to by far the largest part of the National
Party's income ; the relation of revenue from this
source to total general fund income from all sources
(including loans) during the last thirteen years for
which figures are given in Party Conference Reports
follows :

LABOUR PARTY INCOME, 1924-36
Affiliation Fees

Year	Total Income	Total Affiliation Fees	Unions and Socialist Societies	Local Parties	Other Sources
	£	£	£	£	£
1924	48,769	37,269	36,079	1,190	11,500
1925	64,082	40,942	39,563	1,379	23,140
1926	64,366	58,105	55,774	2,331	6,261
1927	50,045	40,622	38,949	1,673	9,423
1928	48,614	35,414	33,325	2,089	13,200
1929	48,142	28,955	26,949	2,006	19,187
1930	46,409	41,404	35,781	5,623	5,005
1931	48,971	35,891	31,695	4,196	13,080
1932	45,689	39,291	33,898	5,393	6,398
1933	41,311	38,438	32,588	5,850	2,873
1934	38,417	38,075	31,640	6,436	342
1935	40,217	39,580	32,689	6,891	637
1936	44,336	40,863	33,589	7,274	3,473

In 1918 the national affiliation fee was raised from
one to two pence, and in 1920 from two to three pence.
An increasingly heavy load of central administrative
expenses and grants to local Parties made necessary the
decision of the 1925 Conference to collect double levy
for one year only, which accounts for the high peak of

affiliation fee collections in 1926. The 1929 Conference authorized a special twopence levy spread over three years, and raised the regular affiliation fee to fourpence. The increase of the regular fee to fourpence halfpenny went into effect in 1937. The contributions from Socialist societies (which are grouped with the Trade Unions) have been small ; likewise grouped with the Trade Unions are the contributions of the Royal Arsenal Co-operative Society, which ranged from £400 in 1929 to £600 in 1936.

The greatest portion of Party expenditures, however, is made in the constituencies, in preparation for and in the conduct of Election campaigns. The money-raising activities of local Parties will be examined in some detail in a subsequent chapter. It will suffice to say here that Constituency Parties receive the greatest part of their funds from four sources : (1) individual membership fees ; (2) affiliation fees paid through local branches of Trade Unions and Co-operative societies ; (3) the Trade Union or other group which may have assumed financial responsibility for the constituency candidate ; (4) and a variety of bazaars, entertainments, and other money-raising schemes.

No accurate data are available on the total amounts raised and spent by local Parties. However, it may be estimated that each individual member contributes an average of about two shillings and sixpence yearly. At this rate, the Party's 430,694 members affiliated through local Parties must contribute nearly £55,000 in membership fees. This total would mean the average organized Constituency Party would have about £100 in membership income. Special drives and social events would increase this average by another £100 per Party, or an estimated total of £110,000 raised by local Labour Parties. The funds of Socialist and Professional societies might amount to £5,000.

Local Parties are the largest spending agencies of the Labour Party. They spend not only nearly all of their own funds, but also large amounts contributed by the Trade Unions for local affiliation fees, special donations for various purposes, and constituency " nursing " on behalf of Trade Union candidates.

B. POLITICAL FUNDS OF LABOUR'S ALLIES : THE TRADE UNIONS AND THE CO-OPERATIVE PARTY

Perhaps the greatest part of funds expended in behalf of the Labour Party are raised by the Trade Unions through their political levies. The rate of the political levy varies considerably from Union to Union. In 1934, the National Union of Railwaymen and the National Union of Distributive and Allied Workers, for example, collected individual contributions of about two shillings per " contracting in " member[1] ; the total British Trade Unionists who paid the political levy that year subscribed an average of about one shilling and sixpence ; smaller Unions like the National Society of Pottery Workers, often collect an annual political levy of one shilling. The average yearly political expenditure by all Trade Unions during 1932-4 inclusive was just under £140,000. In the

General Election years of 1931 and 1935, £217,000 and £229,000 were spent. The Registrar of Friendly Societies has summarized the combined political fund figures for all Unions, registered and unregistered, during the last eight years available as follows[2] :

TRADE UNION POLITICAL FUNDS, 1928-35

Year	Number contributing £	Contributions £	Expenditures £	Funds at End of Year £
1928	2,088,000	170,000	201,000	413,000
1929	2,119,000	159,000	218,000	369,000
1930	2,144,000	168,000	138,000	412,000
1931	2,045,000	144,000	217,000	351,000
1932	1,916,000	151,000	131,000	386,000
1933	1,915,000	145,000	144,000	406,000
1934	1,983,000	157,000	143,000	432,000
1935	2,078,000	163,000	229,000	378,000

These figures include a few small associations of traders and employers. Their contributions and expenditures are insignificant, but the total reserve for 1935 includes £67,000 held by the National Farmers' Union, a union of employers.

The political fund reserves held by Trade Unions are chiefly in the hands of the more powerful groups ; at the end of 1935 the National Union of Railwaymen had £104,000, the National Union of General and Municipal Workers had £32,000, the Durham Miners' Association had £39,000, and the Mineworkers' Federation of Great Britain held £34,000. This rather large reserve of political funds was built up in the years when Trade Unionism had a higher membership than

at present, and before the effect of the Trades Disputes
and Trades Union Act of 1927 had reduced the number
of contributors to the political fund. During recent
years the expenditures have been above contributions,
but reserves have been maintained by the income from
interest on investments.

The political funds of the Trade Unions are spent for
(1) affiliation fees to the National Party, (2) the
subscriptions of branches to local Labour Parties,
(3) contributions to national, local, and special
campaign funds, (4) financing Trade Union candidates
in particular constituencies, (5) expenses of delegates
to Labour Conferences, (6) in some Unions, compensation of individuals for the loss of wages while serving in
municipal office, and (7) political propaganda efforts
both of the Party and the Union.

Before 1927, every Trade Unionist belonging to a
Union affiliated to the Labour Party automatically
became a member of the Party, unless he requested
exemption (" contracted out ").   Under the 1927 Act,
only Trade Unionists who specifically express in
writing a desire to contribute to the political fund
become members of the Labour Party (" contracted
in ").

After the basis of collection of the political levy was
altered from " contracting out " to " contracting in ",
the number of contributors dropped at once.   In 1927,
the last year of the " contracting out " plan, over
three-fourths of British Trade Unionists contributed to
political funds.   During the first four years of the Act's
operation, 1928 to 1932, an average of only fifty-nine

per cent. of members in "registered" Unions "contracted in". By 1935, the percentage had dropped to fifty-six. Labour Party finances have never fully recovered from this severe blow.

The Co-operative Party is so closely allied with the Labour Party in both the constituencies and Parliament that its expenditures must be considered with those of the Trade Unions and local Parties. Affiliation fees were paid by member societies, retail and wholesale, for more than five million members, amounting to nearly £11,000 in 1935 ; and at the beginning of 1936 the Co-operative Party had a balance in hand of over £12,000.[3] Its funds are spent for national propaganda and organization, for regional organizers, and for local work in constituencies where approved Co-operators have been adopted as joint Labour and Co-operative candidates. In addition, Co-operative societies commonly subsidize local Parties or Political Councils which are often affiliated to the local Labour Parties. The two great societies operating in the London area have a combined membership of about 900,000, and had political budgets in one year (1934-5) of over £23,000, as will be shown subsequently. Other British Co-operatives do not make proportionate political expenditures, but the total cost of Co-operative political activities must amount to £50,000 or more yearly.

C. Special Funds of the Labour Party

The Labour Party handles a few special funds requiring separate treatment. The largest of these is the General Election Fund, which is raised by special appeals from individual and organizational sources. It has never been comparable in size to the Election funds of the other two major Parties.   Special appeals have been made at each of the recent General Elections, and the following amounts collected[4] :

			£
1923	..	..	32,500
1924	..	..	28,500
1929	..	..	49,200
1931	..	..	30,000
1935	..	..	21,800

Between one-third and one-half of the Election funds raised for both the 1929 and 1931 Elections has been used for general fund or normal Party administration purposes, a practice which has been necessitated by the inadequate sums available for headquarters use since 1928.   The 1935 fund was used for the Election campaign ;   around £15,800 was granted to constituencies.   The Election services financed by these funds are grants to constituencies, expenses of national speakers, printing of the Election manifesto and other campaign literature.   More than one-half of the 1935 fund was contributed by Trade Unions.

The Insurance Deposit Fund was established in 1929 for the purpose of pooling among all the Constituency Parties which put up Labour candidates in General Elections the risk of losing Returning Officers' deposits. A guarantee against the forfeiture of the £150 deposit required of each candidate is of particular value in the numerous constituencies where Labour is weakest, and where there is always a risk that the required one-eighth of all votes polled may not be obtained. Under this scheme the Party requires a premium of ten pounds to be paid on behalf of each candidate. If the candidate's deposit is forfeited, the fund returns the £150.

Twenty deposits were lost in 1931 and sixteen in 1935 ; after both Elections there was a considerable balance left in the fund. Endorsements were withheld by the Executive from twelve candidates who in 1931 failed to pay the insurance premium. A more satisfactory unanimity was obtained in 1935. Nearly all of the insurance fund was loaned to the general fund in 1932 and never returned, a rather indefensible procedure which makes the premium a sort of a head tax on Constituency Parties irrespective of size and ability to pay. The balance of £3,130 remaining after the 1935 Election was appropriated for use in organizing rural and semi-rural areas.

The By-Election Insurance Fund was established by the 1932 Conference to spread the financial burden of by-elections over the whole of the Party's affiliated membership, superseding an earlier special election fund raised by a voluntary levy on local Parties only. Under the present scheme, all Constituency Parties pay an equal premium, and the nationally affiliated organizations contribute according to their size, being classed for the purpose into seven groups. Collections and grants for by-elections during the last few years have ranged from £225 to £500 per contest. Although this application of the insurance principle to by-elections has lifted a part of the heavy burden from Constituency Parties and placed it more fairly on all of the affiliated bodies, small Parties often encounter difficulty in raising their allotments. This scheme has caused these important special contests to be fought with more adequate funds and organization than formerly, and has also strengthened somewhat the authority of the Executive in the selection of candidates.

A number of special funds have been established by the Party for particular purposes. The " Victory for Socialism " Fund is the most important carried on the Party's books in recent years. It was set up to finance a propaganda campaign to expound Party policy and increase membership. A total of £8,641 was raised by appeals to the usual sources—the Trade Unions, local Parties, and individuals.

The Party has a large sale of its own publications, leaflets, and propaganda which is not shown in the above accounts. Unlike most political Parties, the Labour Party sells nearly all of its literature. This is done in part through necessity, for the funds of the Party are rigidly limited, and partly because local Parties have been found to make more effective use of literature for which they have paid the cost of printing and delivery. The joint Party-Trades Union Congress organ, *Labour*, the League of Youth magazine, *New Nation*, and *Weekly Notes for Speakers* all have been published at a loss, but the *Labour Woman* has made a modest profit during the last four years. Due chiefly to losses on propaganda leaflets, posters, pamphlets, etc., the literature account usually shows a deficit which must be made up from general funds.

D. Estimated Aggregate Expenditures on behalf of Labour Politics

An American investigator, Professor James K. Pollock, has estimated that an average of £300,000 is spent by or for the Labour Party yearly, assuming one General Election every three years.[5] Pollock estimated that the Conservatives spent £600,000 yearly and the Liberals £400,000. It is possible that this was about the amount spent for Labour during the period the material for his study was collected (before 1931), but it is doubtful if during the period 1932 to 1937 an average political expenditure of less than £330,000 yearly has been made by all Party agencies and allies, including the national and local Parties, Trade Unions, and Co-operatives, and assuming a General Election every four years.

In summary, this amount may be estimated roughly by sources : Trade Unions furnish annually for political purposes about £160,000 ; Co-operative agencies contribute about £50,000 yearly ; local Labour Parties raise approximately £110,000, and Socialist societies, £5,000 ; perhaps £5,000 additional are raised from individuals and miscellaneous sources.

The average yearly expenditure of this £330,000 may be estimated also by spending agencies. The National Labour Party spends around £50,000 for ordinary and special purposes, not including Elections. Co-operative politicians expend about £40,000.

Co-operative political spending is less than income both because a considerable sum is spent for the affiliation of local Co-operative groups with local Labour Parties and because a reserve is being accumulated by the Co-operative Party. About £160,000 are spent regularly by or through the local Parties. Part of this sum is contributed by Trade Unions. Its expenditure often is directed to constituencies choosing Trade Union candidates for Parliament.

Approximately £50,000 of Labour's General Election expenses should be allocated to each year. The Home Office's official report on expenses in the 1931 Election revealed that an aggregate expenditure of £654,105 was reported by all candidates in that Election ; of this amount, endorsed Labour candidates spent a grand total of £181,629.

Endorsed Labour candidates in the 1935 campaign returned aggregate expenditures of £196,819 out of a grand total of £722,093 for all candidates. For contested constituencies, the average Labour expenditure was £364 per candidate. A striking difference exists in the amounts spent for candidates financed by local Labour Parties, on the one hand, and those financed by Trade Unions or the Co-operative Party, on the other. Divisional Parties fought the 1935 Election on an average of £302 ; average Trade Union sponsored candidates spent £551 ; Co-operative Party candidates averaged £548 expended on their behalf.

National and other non-reportable expenditures would bring this total to over £200,000 for both 1931 and 1935 Elections, which may be taken as typical so

far as total Labour Party expenditures are concerned.
Since 1924, British General Elections have occurred at
average intervals of four years.   Allocated accordingly,
£50,000 yearly should be charged off to each year for
General Election expenses.   The balance, £30,000, is
spent chiefly for municipal elections and for Trade
Union political expenditures not included in the above.

Total expenditures on behalf of Labour politics
probably are adequate to finance a major British
political Party, given the large amount of voluntary
work done for the Labour Party.   But the allocation
of these funds is spotted and unbalanced.   Two chief
sources of funds, the Trade Unions and the Co-
operatives, insist upon either spending their money
directly or upon supervising its expenditure through a
Constituency Party which has chosen one of their own
for a parliamentary candidate.   Until the Unions and
Co-operatives are willing to pool a larger part of their
political funds for common endeavours, Labour
finances probably cannot be placed on a satisfactory
basis.

E.   The Work and Authority of the Central Organizing Staff

The organizing staff of the Labour Party is under the
direction of the National Agent, Mr G. R. Shepherd,
who is advised by the organization sub-committee of
the Executive.   Since the period of rapid expansion
following the war, field work has been carried on by a
staff of nine district organizers and nine women
organizers, operating in pairs in the nine districts into

which Britain is divided for organizational purposes. These districts are : North-Eastern, North-Western, Midlands, Home and Southern, London, South-Western, Eastern, Wales and Monmouth, Scotland.

Four propagandists were retained for special work until the Party's financial difficulties which followed the Trades Disputes and Trades Union Act of 1927 made it necessary to reduce this number to two, then, in 1932, to discontinue the work altogether. Since then one or two staff men have devoted their time between propaganda and League of Youth work. During special campaigns, additional propagandists generally are added to the staff on a temporary basis.

The regular work of the organizing staff consists of day to day contact with and guidance of the local Parties, booking speakers and arranging conferences, campaigns, and membership drives, conducting by-elections, organizing Labour Parties in the " backward " areas of rural Britain, training and examining Constituency Party Agents, and planning and directing centrally the Party's propaganda efforts. Several of these functions are carried out with the co-operation of other headquarters departments, but the chief responsibility for their execution lies in the organizing staff.

The authority of the Head Office in the constituencies is derived in part from powers expressly granted in the Party Constitution, and in part from the natural desires of the local groups for direction. The Party Constitution places many obligations on the Executive which the Executive, in turn, delegates to the

Organization Department. The Constitution requires the Executive to see that local Parties are established in every constituency. The Executive may expel individual members or disaffiliate organizations in enforcing the Constitution, Standing Orders, and Rules of the Party, a power which has been invoked repeatedly when members or local Parties have appeared to come under Communist influence. Under a system of grants-in-aid, the National Party helps local Parties meet the salaries of full-time Agents. The right to endorse individual candidates for Parliament gives to the Executive a veto over one of the most important functions of the Divisional Parties. All local Parties are required to organize along lines laid down in the " Model Rules " approved by the 1929 Conference.

But the Central Office has other powers and duties which flow inherently from its position. It has the prestige attached to the national agency of the Party ; it can provide speakers of importance for local meetings ; it has the full-time skilled personnel necessary to carry on sustained campaigns for propaganda and organizational purposes.

F. RELATION OF CONSTITUENCY AGENTS TO THE CENTRAL OFFICE

Constituency Agents look to the Head Office not only for training and certification, but also for the future advancement of their professional status through their organization, the National Union of Labour Organizers and Election Agents. This Union issues a small monthly publication, the *Labour Organizer*, which is edited by one of the Party district organizers. An adjustments board composed of four representatives of the Executive and four of the Agents' Union meets occasionally to discuss salary questions and proposals for superannuation schemes.

The Party Organization Department conducts series of correspondence study courses on elections, publicity, and organization. Notes and folios are issued monthly to those who enrol in the course ; a charge is made for each one enrolled ; local Parties and Trade Union branches are urged to assist. At the end of the training period, an examination is given in various centres. A very high proportion of entrants pass the examination and receive diplomas.

Since 1917 the national organization has assisted in financing the employment of full-time Agents in the constituencies. By 1922 grants-in-aid expenditures for this purpose reached over £5,500, but the subsidies were gradually decreased under a scheme approved by the 1926 Conference. Under the revised plan, fifteen per cent. of that part of the Agent's salary actually raised by the Constituency Party, after deducting any funds furnished by an individual candidate or sponsoring organization, was granted by the National Party. Lack of funds caused the Executive to reduce the grant to ten per cent. in 1932 and 1933.

The 1933 Conference approved another scheme under which no further local Parties could enter the old system of grants-in-aid. In its place a plan of development grants was set up for constituencies without Agents and without adequate funds. A sharply graduated scale of payments was made available, starting with fifteen per cent. in the first year and expiring after the third year's grant of five per cent. The Executive was given authority to make other grants in special cases. Under the fifteen per cent. arrangement, £2,440 were paid out to local Parties in 1931 ; under the ten per cent. plan, £2,218 were paid in 1932, and £1,290 in 1933 ; with the new scheme in effect in 1934, only £953 were made in grants ; in 1935, £774 ; in 1936, £1,103.

G. Women and Youth in the Party Organization

Since the war much of the Labour Party's organizing efforts have been devoted to women. They received special attention from the Party because their enfranchisement in 1918 and 1928 more than doubled the size of the electorate. In 1918, 13,000,000 new voters came on the Register, chiefly through the enfranchisement of women over thirty years of age. In 1928, 5,000,000 were added by the extension of the franchisement to women on equal terms with men.

It was felt that the general Party approach through Trade Unions and the usual channels was not enough, but that special efforts must be made to enlist women Party workers through semi-social activities. This Labour has done with notable success. Women are represented separately in nearly every phase of Party organization. An additional woman delegate may be sent to the Conference by a local Party with a membership in excess of 2,500. There are five places specifically designated for women on the National Executive.

Women's work is directed by the Chief Woman Officer in the Central Office and there is a woman organizer in each of the nine organizational divisions in the United Kingdom. The Party publishes a monthly journal, the *Labour Woman*, which especially is designed to appeal to women. Much of the women's organizing work revolves around the annual National Conference of Labour Women, composed of delegates from women's sections in local Parties and women's groups of other organizations affiliated with the Labour Party. Recent women's conferences were attended by 500 to 600 delegates, largely from local Party women's sections, although women Trade Unionists, Trade Union women's guilds, Co-operative societies, and Socialist societies were also represented.

The chief business on the Conference agenda centres around reports from the Standing Joint Committee of Industrial Women's Organizations. This Committee is composed of women from the Labour Party, Trade Unions, Co-operative societies, and Socialist groups. It acts both as adviser on women's affairs to the Party Executive, and in the capacity of spokesman for working class women on women's industrial welfare, maternity services, child health, education, and other matters. The work of women's groups in local Labour Parties is examined in a subsequent chapter.

Recently, by a special approach, the Party has attempted to interest young people in its work. The Labour Party League of Youth admits, as members, individual Party members between the ages of sixteen and twenty-one years. From 1929 to 1936 an annual

Conference of delegates from League branches was held, but the Conference was not permitted to discuss policy. Until 1937 the chairman of each Conference sat as an *ex officio* member of the Party's National Executive for the subsequent year and also served with one other League of Youth representative as an *ex officio* delegate to the Party Conference. It was affiliated with the Socialist Youth International and the National Workers' Sport Association. A small monthly magazine, the *New Nation*, was issued by the Central Office. The Executive reported, in 1935, that 526 branches of the Youth organization were in existence.

Disturbing tendencies in the League of Youth reached a crisis in 1936. According to the Executive's report to the Conference, leaders in the Youth group sought to decide matters of policy, substantial independence for the organization, and a united front with Communist Youth groups. These considerations led the Executive to recommend and the Conference to endorse a drastic reorganization of the League of Youth, narrowing the age limits, disbanding the League advisory committee, suspending publication of the *New Nation*, and cancelling Youth Conferences. Subsequent attempts have been made to revive the League, but apparently little success has marked such efforts. The 1937 Party Conference ordered an early Conference of League of Youth branches to plan its future.

H. SPECIAL NATIONAL CAMPAIGNS

Special organizational and propaganda campaigns occupy an important place in the work of the

Party Central Office. The first type has as its goal strengthening of Party machinery and increasing membership. Series of organizational conferences for all Party workers are held nearly every year. Various problems of local organization are discussed at each. Many individual membership campaigns were conducted between 1931 and 1937; in some the country was divided into several regions and a mass conference was held in each; in others, particular constituencies were chosen for intensive campaigns. These drives have proven successful in building up membership, forming new Parties, reviving moribund ones, and instructing local Party officers in organizational techniques.

Labour's difficulty in organizing rural constituencies has prompted a second type of special effort, campaigns to increase Trade Union and Labour Party membership in the rural areas. Since 1932 the Party has joined with the National Union of Agricultural Workers, the Transport and General Workers' Union, and the *Daily Herald* in annual drives to build up membership and support in selected agricultural constituencies. The greatly increased Labour voting strength in rural areas in the 1935 Election may be attributed in part to these intensive campaigns, which in themselves constitute a dramatic chapter in Party history.

Propaganda campaigns to explain and expound Labour Party policy declarations constitute a third category of special effort. Included in this classification are the " Call to Action " campaign of 1932-3,

" Victory for Socialism" in 1934-5, "The Great Betrayal" on the League of Nations issue in 1935-6, and the drive launching "Labour's Immediate Programme" especially as presented in the attractive pamphlet "Your Britain". In most of these special propaganda efforts, tons of literature were distributed through Party machinery, numerous meetings, demonstrations, and rallies were held throughout the country, intensive work was done in the constituencies. Sometimes special money-raising drives are conducted to finance the campaigns ; over £8,600 were raised for " Victory for Socialism ". Other propaganda efforts are financed from regular sources.

CHAPTER THREE

REFERENCES

1 National Union of Railwaymen *Report and Financial Statements for 1934* (London, 1935), p. 5 ; National Union of Distributive and Allied Workers *Statistics, 1934* (London, 1935), p. 28.

2 *Report of the Chief Registrar of Friendly Societies, 1936,* Part 4, Trade Unions (London, 1937), p. 13.

3 *Annual Report of the Co-operative Party to the National Conference, 1936* (Manchester, 1936), pp. 2-3.

4 *1929 Conference,* p. 220 ; *1932 Conference,* p. 58 ; *1936 Conference,* p. 103.

5 James K. Pollock, *Money and Politics Abroad* (New York, 1932), p. 25.

CHAPTER FOUR

THE CENTRAL OFFICE :
PROPAGANDA, RESEARCH AND INTER-
NATIONAL PROBLEMS

A. PRESS RELATIONS

THE routine work of the Labour Party's Press and
Publicity Department, headed by Mr. W. W. Henderson, consists of day to day contacts with newspaper
correspondents, both British and foreign. During
sessions of Parliament, an assistant handles parliamentary news directly through the House of Commons
press gallery and lobby correspondents. In addition
to daily releases to metropolitan and larger provincial
newspapers, a regular weekly " Labour Press Service "
is issued to country newspapers, periodicals, and local
Party organs. The weekly service includes an
editorial of general interest and some account of the
chief news items of the week. In general, the treatment
of news by the Party department is quite objective.
International and League of Nations matters receive
much attention. Statements of the Party Executive
and the National Council of Labour are issued with a
minimum of partisan comment.

This discreetness of approach is made necessary by
the almost uniform hostility of the British press toward
the Labour Party. By tactful handling, the support
of the " capitalist press " is obtained to publicize
Labour views on certain specific and immediate

problems between elections. For example, the aid of Liberal newspapers like the *Manchester Guardian* and the *News Chronicle* has been given to the Labour Party in its fight against the National Government's policy of protection ; several Conservative papers joined the Party in urging a strong British lead in the League sanctions movement ; even Lord Beaverbrook, an arch enemy of Socialism, throws the support of his powerful newspaper chain behind Labour's demand for high wages.

There is a remarkable concentration of ownership of the British press, with a handful of groups controlling not only the London newspapers, but those of the provincial cities as well. As in America, the modern newspaper, a development of improved printing machinery, cheap paper supply, mass production, and advertising, has become a huge business concern.[1] Britain's two leading newspapers, *The Times* and the *Manchester Guardian*, however, are independents ; although both have comparatively small circulations (estimated in 1936 at 187,000 and 50,000 respectively), they exert a very great influence because of their accuracy and maturity.

The real competition in England is in the one penny field, where the giants of newspaperdom struggle to build up and maintain enormous circulations by free gifts, free family insurance, crossword puzzles and guessing contests, some with prizes of £10,000 and more. Three chief groups, the Beaverbrook, the Rothermere, and the Berry, virtually dominate the field with sensational, cheap papers. Listed in order of their circulations, the essential data concerning the leading London penny morning newspapers in 1936 were as follows :[2]

Newspaper	Politics	Circulation	Proprietors
Daily Herald	Labour	2,000,000	T.U.C & Odhams, Ltd.
Daily Express	Tory	1,911,000	Beaverbrook
Daily Mail	Tory	1,689,000	Rothermere
News Chronicle	Liberal	1,348,000	Cadbury family
Daily Mirror	Tory	1,000,000	Rothermere
Daily Sketch	Tory	1,000,000	Berry
Daily Telegraph	Tory	445,000	Berry

The evening press is more limited, but the same groups control the three leading papers :[2]

Newspaper	Politics	Circulation	Proprietors
Evening News	Tory	728,000	Rothermere
Evening Star	Liberal	477,000	Cadbury family
Evening Standard	Tory	400,000	Beaverbrook

B. The *DAILY HERALD*

It is surprising that the Labour Movement's organ, the *Daily Herald*, should be setting the pace in circulation ; but it was the first paper in Britain to reach a circulation of two million, a daily record now maintained for more than four years. Launched in 1912 with a small capital and the inspiration of George Lansbury and a few others, the paper has managed to survive. The interesting story of the early days of the *Herald* was told by George Lansbury in *The Miracle of Fleet Street*. During the war period, it was published successfully as a weekly, but financial difficulties returned when it was restarted as a daily in 1919. Although it was critical of the official policy of the

Party and advocated the cause of the Marxist "left wing", large amounts of money were raised in the Labour Movement to keep the *Herald* going.

In 1922, the Labour Party and the Trades Union Congress jointly took over the paper. A good start was made, but the Party found the burden too heavy and was forced to withdraw, leaving the Trades Union Congress with both the losing newspaper and the Victoria House Printing Company, Ltd., a fairly successful printing plant. The losses continued to be heavy, however, and the Trades Union Congress negotiated and formed a partnership called "Daily Herald, Ltd.", with Odhams Press, Ltd., a large commercial firm.[3] Odham's had modern presses for their Sunday paper, *The People*, and recognized the advantages of utilizing them in the production of a daily for the eight million Labour voters previously without an adequate daily press.

This strange partnership has been a remarkable business success. Under the terms of the agreement, the business policy and profits are under the control of Odhams, which has fifty-one per cent. of the stock and five directors, but the political and industrial policies are dictated by the Trades Union Congress, which holds forty-nine per cent. of the stock and has four directors. On the day the new arrangement came in force, March 17th, 1930, the circulation was raised from 250,000 to 1,000,000 ; by September 1932 it reached 1,600,000 ; in July 1933 it achieved the high goal of 2,000,000, and then claimed "the largest daily net sale in the world".

Actually the *Herald* is little, if any, superior to its competitors ; it is popularly written, with a considerable tendency to the spectacular. Neither the foreign nor the domestic news is reported as well as in *The Times* or *Guardian,* or the better American papers. Its parliamentary reporting is fair, although there are some justifiable complaints that the debates are not given in sufficient detail. The *Daily Herald's* pages contain a great deal of advertising of patent medicines and cheap merchandise. Excellent feature and editorial pages compensate for the weaker sections. The *Herald* outdoes its competitors in offering gifts and prizes of enormous size ; its free insurance policy pays benefits up to £10,000 for certain accidents.

From the point of view of the Party, however, the new business status of the *Herald* is more satisfactory than under any previous arrangement. There is no longer a diversion of individual, Trade Union, or Party funds to the paper. A total of £36,000 of Party funds went to the *Herald* between 1922 and the Party's withdrawal from the partnership. The circulation has reached a figure of about five times the maximum ever reached under previous control. The *Herald* is a very great help in campaign times : for by-elections, it issues special editions carrying pictures and local news of the contest ; for General and local Elections, it gives constant support and publicity to the Labour cause ; during special campaigns it provides leaflets, equipment and becomes a medium of communication. There are several regular editions issued daily from the London and Manchester plants, each one adapted to the special interests of a particular region, and furnishing localized Party news to Labour adherents in the various communities.

C. Sunday Newspapers and "Left" Periodicals

Among the Sunday newspapers, only *Reynold's News*, now owned by the Co-operative Movement through the Co-operative Press, Ltd., actively supports the Labour Party. This is a most important field, because it is generally considered that Sunday newspapers receive much more leisurely and careful reading than dailies, and their aggregate circulation exceeds that of all morning papers. Although *Reynold's* appears in the lower circulation group, an expansion and improvement of the paper's scope and size which was made in March 1936, eventually should increase it materially. The essential data about the leading Sunday papers may be summarized as follows :[4]

Newspaper	Politics	Circulation	Proprietors
News of the World	Independent	3,350,000	Independent
The People	Independent	3,000,000	Odhams, Ltd.
Empire News (*Manchester*)	Tory	1,535,000	Berry
Sunday Pictorial	Tory	1,400,000	Rothermere
Sunday Express	Tory	1,225,000	Beaverbrook
Sunday Chronicle	Tory	900,000	Berry
Sunday Dispatch	Tory	870,000	Rothermere
Reynold's News	Co-operative	400,000	Co-operative
Sunday Times	Tory	235,000	Berry
Observer	Tory	215,000	Independent

The Sunday papers are less unfavourable to Labour than are the dailies. Neither of the two with the largest circulation devotes much attention to politics ; *The People*, published by the co-owners of the *Herald*, is not unfriendly to the Party.

Outside the daily and Sunday newspaper field are several periodicals which contribute materially to the Labour cause. The Glasgow *Forward* is a well written and widely read Socialist weekly ; the *New Leader*, weekly organ of the Independent Labour Party, is still circulating in the Movement ; the *Daily Worker*, issued by the Communist Party, has recently adopted a conciliatory attitude toward the Labour Party, and non-Communist readers who scan its columns probably outnumber its Communist subscribers.

The *New Statesman and Nation*, a magazine of Fabian origin, fills the role of the " intellectual " organ among the Socialist weeklies. The Communist *Labour Monthly* contains critical comment on the official Labour programme. The Party's own *Labour Magazine* and its research publication, *Labour Bulletin*, were merged in September 1933 into a joint Party and Trades Union Congress publication, *Labour*, a monthly which contains news of both the political and industrial movements and articles on various problems and policies of the Party.

The *Clarion*, the survival of the famous organ edited by Robert Blatchford, has been published independently under various auspices. As the *New Clarion*, it was issued from 1932 to 1934 by a company controlled by Victoria House, and at last died in the hands of

Odham's Press, Ltd., joint owners of the *Daily Herald*.
From 1932 it was a twopenny weekly, and devoted its
pages to free and pointed criticism and discussion of
Labour's policy and tactics. Some of the most useful
and productive debates within the Party were carried
on in the *Clarion* between 1931 and 1934. The
Political Quarterly falls more in the class of learned
publications, but its editors are well-known Labourites,
and the " left " bias is evident throughout its well
edited pages. There are a number of Socialist journals
which are issued independently or by small factions,
but none of them is of any great importance to the
Party. Since mid-1936, the Left Book Club's *Left News*
has assumed an important role and an impressive
circulation.

D. The Wireless and the Cinema in British Politics

The wireless is a second important instrument of
propaganda. Unlike the American plan of regulated
private enterprise, British broadcasting is a national
monopoly operated by the British Broadcasting
Corporation, a State agency in the Post Office, and
financed by a tax on receiving sets. The extent of
radio receiving set ownership is indicated accurately
by the number of wireless licenses issued. On
March 31st, 1932, 1934, and 1936 respectively, the
B.B.C. reported 4,624,153, 6,254,428, and 7,617,797
licensed receiving sets in the country.

Very few political addresses are broadcast. During
a General Election campaign, time is allocated among

the political Parties by the Government. This may be fairly divided, as in 1935, when the Government took five periods, Labour was given four, and the Liberals received three, or it may be unproportionately allocated, as in 1931, when Government Parties took eleven broadcasts, giving Labour three and opposition Liberals one—thereby arousing bitter criticisms from the opposition Parties.

During the " General Strike " of 1926, the Government made extensive and effective use of the radio, refusing to allow Trade Union leaders to speak, and unceasingly putting forward the employer-Government case. A feeling persists in the Labour Movement that the news broadcasts on political and Trade Union affairs are of " tendencious " character. Lacking any reporting agency of its own, the British Broadcasting Corporation must, its critics allege, draw from newspaper and Press services, the overwhelming majority of which are anti-Socialist. In general, the Party regards the present state of broadcasting as unsatisfactory, and it aims for the present to correct, by protests, some of the alleged discrimination and to make certain character changes next time it holds office.

In June 1936 the Government issued a " White Paper " declaring its policy regarding broadcasting and announcing its decision on specific recommendations of the Broadcasting Committee of 1935, headed by Lord Ullswater. After declaring its support of the committee's recommendation for renewing of the British Broadcasting Corporation's charter for ten years, the Government reaffirmed its stand against the broadcasting of editorial comment on current affairs. Significantly, the Government rejected the committee's proposal for the appointment of a Minister to be " responsible for broad questions of policy and culture " on the grounds that he might be drawn into exercising actual control. The National Council of Labour had urged upon the committee the necessity of having a Minister freed from heavy departmental duties in charge of the non-technical side of broadcasting.

A third important method of influencing public opinion, the cinema, has not been employed directly against the Labour Party, but there is some evidence that both English and American feature films have an anti-Labour bias. Some of the recent British-made " documentary " films on various problems such as planning, housing, and mining, have behind them a " philosophy of social education " which is in harmony with certain phases of the Labour programme. The newsreels give little notice to any but the most ceremonial political occasions, except during General Election time, when, as in 1935, the chief Labour leaders were not stressed and a few flash close-ups of back benchers were used. Recently, a number of motion pictures have been made by the Socialist Film Council, but they are limited in scope, silent, on sixteen millimetre film, and produced with very small resources. The showing of these films has been limited to Socialist groups and local Parties.

In addition to its attention to the press, the radio, and the cinema, the Labour Party issues a steady and voluminous stream of pamphlets, leaflets, and posters.

The pamphlets, generally, are well written, attractively printed and bound, and sold at very low prices. Recently the Party has issued two excellent pieces of pictorial propaganda. *What Socialism Will Really Mean to You*, a sixteen page rotogravure pamphlet, is profusely illustrated with photographs, graphs, and cartoons. *Your Britain* is an attractive magazine with cover printed in colour, dramatizing in word and picture the " Immediate Programme " of the Labour Party.

Labour's leaflets, however, are no match for the Conservative dodgers, which make direct appeals to the basic emotions. The Labour Party tries to avoid arousing class prejudice, but has failed to find an effective substitute which will make sufficient popular appeal to compete with the numerous diversions available to-day. Labour posters are usually inferior to those of the other Parties, doubtless because of its inability to buy the best art work. It is difficult to see how the Labour Party can evade, without loss, appeal to class antagonisms so long as the Conservative propagandists play upon the fears of the people at Election time.

E. Research for the Labour Party

The Labour Party Research Department is a development of the Party Information Bureau established in 1915, which later became the Joint Research Department for both the Party and the Trades Union Congress and, in 1927, took its present form as the Party's separate research agency. Mr Arthur Greenwood heads the Research Department. It collects statistics and information on various subjects of interest to the Party, answers requests for information on both municipal and national affairs, and issues handbooks and memoranda on a variety of matters. A record of the business interests of Members of the House of Commons and House of Lords is maintained, and data are collected on the financing, profits, and management of business concerns.

In 1936 one of the most important functions of the Research Department was transferred to the newly organized Local Government Department. Thereafter, the services provided for Labour groups on municipal councils have been furnished by this department. Mr G. Grant McKenzie, the member of the research staff who specialized in the municipal field, is in charge of the new local government service.

In the past, regional meetings on municipal problems have been held under Labour Party auspices and have been well attended by Labour members of various Borough, County, and Urban District councils. About fifty representatives of local authorities were present at a Conference on housing in June 1934, at Sheffield, where a Labour majority on the Council was carrying out a bold rehousing programme. Since the Party lacks a definite municipal policy, Labour Councillors for different cities often find fruitful the discussion of their respective problems. The Local Government Department had extensive responsibilities in planning and writing reports of the Party's Distressed Areas Commission, which during 1936-7 did excellent work in investigating and focusing attention on the situation of the special areas.

The defeat of nearly every Labour front bencher in the 1931 Election left in the House of Commons a small group of forty-six Labour Members, most of whom were inadequately trained to debate intelligently the complicated issues involved in the National Government's legislative programme. The situation meant that the experienced parliamentarians—Lansbury, Attlee, Cripps, and (after 1932) Greenwood—were forced to carry a very heavy burden in the House. Other less skilled Members were furnished with briefs, memoranda, and materials by the Research Department, and by applying themselves to the subject at hand, were able to make suitable presentations of Labour's case on fields formerly unfamiliar to them.

The period intervening between the General Elections of 1931 and 1935 was marked by the re-framing of Labour Party policy. This restatement of aims was carried out under the direction of a sub-committee of the Executive, and framed by four sub-committees consisting of members of the Executive and co-opted specialists. The Research Department was responsible for the preparation of memoranda and reports for the sub-committees, did most of the drafting of the reports, and provided the secretarial work.

A number of Party pamphlets are prepared or edited by members of the research staff. Until 1933 the department issued a monthly publication, the *Labour Bulletin*, which contained a variety of data on industrial and political problems, and devoted considerable attention to municipal matters. Since the *Bulletin* has been combined with other organs to form the joint monthly magazine, *Labour*, the department has contributed occasional special articles on municipal and national problems. Much research material collected goes into the propaganda leaflets and news releases issued through other agencies of the Party. Research reports issued by the Party's department are often lengthy and may be unnecessarily involved.

The Library maintained jointly by the Party and the Trades Union Congress has an excellent collection of domestic and foreign periodicals. All London dailies and three French newspapers are clipped and filed regularly ; the three staff librarians index all articles marked by the various Party and Trades Union Congress departments. Only a limited supply of books on political and industrial subjects has been collected.

The Party Research Department is frequently confused with the Labour Research Department, now allegedly under Communist control. Organized in 1912, this agency was known as the Fabian Research Department, and worked in close conjunction with the Labour Party. It assumed the name Labour Research Department in 1918 and moved into the Party headquarters. A number of distinguished Fabians took a leading part in its work. Since 1921-2, when the joint Research Department of the Party and the Trades Union Congress was established, the Labour Research

Department has operated independently, but some of its leaders have become prominent members of the Communist Party. In spite of its radical connections, however, the agency has managed to survive on the subscriptions of Trade Unions and Co-operative societies, and continues to publish a monthly periodical, *Labour Research*, which contains numerous interesting data on corporation profits, salaries, and other matters which in general are presented more attractively and issued in more convenient form than reports of the Party department.

A revival of the independent Fabian spirit of research appears in the New Fabian Research Bureau, established in 1931 by promising young intellectuals under the sponsorship of Party leaders. Its object is to promote inquiry and research into " practical problems of Labour and Socialist policy ", and it is performing a valuable function for the Movement both by publishing the results of its research and by holding meetings and conferences for the discussion of various problems. The Bureau issues a magazine, the *Quarterly Review*, and has published a variety of books and pamphlets which are units of a comprehensive scheme of research in every field of Labour Party policy. Its membership has remained small ; its yearly budget is a modest one of £1,000 ; among its officers and executive committee-men have been a number of distinguished Labour leaders, including Lord Addison, Mrs G. D. H. Cole, Professor Harold J. Laski, Mr C. M. Lloyd, barristers D. H. Pritt and W. A. Robson, and others.

F. International Activities of the Party

Some of the most striking successes of the two Labour Governments were in the field of foreign relations, a fact which may be due in part to the sustained and careful research in international affairs carried on by the Party over a period of many years. The International and Imperial Advisory Committees have conducted investigations on various questions in the field, and issue a number of memoranda every year. Since 1921 there has been an International Department of the Party, responsible for the conduct of the international relations and affairs of the Executive, for translation work for other departments, for contribution of articles on foreign affairs to the Party publications, and, more recently, for co-operation with other organizations in refugee work for victims of Italian, German, and Austrian fascism.

The Labour Party has played a leading role in the international Socialist movement since the Labour Representation Committee days. In 1904 it joined the Second (Socialist) International. After the war, the Party aided in organizing the " Berne International ", and since the 1923 amalgamation with the " Vienna International ", it has been active in the Labour and Socialist International which has its headquarters at Brussels.[5] William Gillies, Secretary of the department, acts as international officer for the Party, and represents it in the bureau and executive committee of the Labour and Socialist International. The British Labour Party had, in 1935, 40 out of 304

6

votes in the Labour and Socialist International, and contributes between £1,200 and £1,800 yearly in affiliation fees.

During the last six years, the department has conducted a number of disarmament demonstrations ; letters of encouragement were sent to the German Social Democratic Party on the eve of the 1932 elections ; two members of the Executive attended an emergency conference of Austrian Socialists in October, 1933 ; delegates were sent to the Czechoslovakian Workers' Olympiad ; a special tour was arranged in the Scandinavian countries.

The work of the International Department assumes even greater importance as fascism becomes more threatening on the continent. Every development in the Spanish situation in 1936-7 was followed closely, and frequent joint executive committee meetings of the Labour and Socialist International and the International Federation of Trade Unions were held.

The work of the International Advisory Committee has been described as " one of the most unique experiments in modern organization of political parties ".[6] The Committee originally was planned as a body of specialists to consider and advise on matters of international character, and to provide material for propaganda and policy declarations. Its work has continued for many years under the same leadership, with C. R. Buxton as Chairman and Leonard S. Woolf as Secretary, and its contributions to the Party have always been of a very high order. Since the fall of the second Labour Government, the Committee has produced memoranda on the Disarmament Conference, the League and Sanctions, the Labour Party and the League, the Locarno Treaties, foreign policy of the National Government, Austria, the Saar, an Eastern Locarno Pact, the naval conversations, the Anglo-German Naval Agreement, the Italo-Abyssinian dispute, the arms race, the reoccupation of the Rhineland, Palestine policy, League Reform, a new Security Agreement, and various colonial matters.

CHAPTER FOUR

REFERENCES

[1] See Herbert Tracey, *The British Press* (London, 1929), pp. 13-16 ; Kurt von Stutterheim, *The Press in England* (London, 1934), pp. 113-71.

[2] Circulation figures furnished by a private advertising agency. Ownership data from *Willing's Press Guide, 1934* (London, April 1934).

[3] R. B. Suthers, " The Daily Herald," *Labour Magazine*, Vol. xi (December 1932), pp. 264-8. The Party was given 55,000 shares of stock in Victoria House and two directors.

[4] Circulation figures obtained from a private advertising agency, 1936. Ownership data from Kingsley Martin, " Public Opinion : The Sunday Newspapers," *Political Quarterly*, Vol. vi (January-March 1935), pp. 111-15.

[5] William P. Maddox, *Foreign Relations in British Labour Politics* (Cambridge Mass., 1934), pp. 21-2.

[6] *Ibid.*, p. 99.

LOCAL ORGANIZATION OF THE LABOUR PARTY

A. THE ROLE OF LOCAL PARTIES IN THE FIGHT FOR POWER

BEFORE 1918 the Labour Party left the basic work of constituency organization to the local branches of the Independent Labour Party, and to the local Trades Councils, which combined the forces of Trade Unionism for local industrial and political action. Under the constitutional changes of 1918, the Party undertook to organize official branches, with which individuals might affiliate directly.

These local Labour Parties took a variety of forms. The key organization is the Constituency Labour Party, which is responsible for the selection of the parliamentary candidate and for the conduct of the Election campaign. In divided Boroughs (with more than one parliamentary constituency), Central Labour Parties are formed to co-ordinate the activities of the various Party organizations within the municipality. Both urban and rural districts usually have a Party organization ; villages and towns commonly have local Parties. There are forty-six or more Federations of Labour Parties, which exist chiefly for the purpose of co-ordinating the work of local Parties in the County and other Elections.

Although the National Party requires them to be organized along lines outlined in model rules approved by the Annual Conference, local Parties still retain a considerable degree of autonomy. Moreover, they are rapidly increasing in membership while the number of affiliated Trade Unionists has declined over a period of years, a tendency which has continued to the extent that the Constituency Parties are demanding a large measure of influence over Party policy. Local Parties do the work of organization, raise and spend a large proportion of Party funds, and contest Elections, for which services they have had a rather small voice in National Party affairs.

Impatient over the comparative impotence of local Parties in the determination of policy and the direction of the Party machine, some minor Party leaders launched a movement in 1933 for the formation of a national "Association of Constituency Labour Parties". Their case was strong. They claimed that the present allocation of Conference voting power solely on the basis of affiliation fees to the National Party is grossly unfair. Although the Trade Unions furnish the greatest part of the Central Office revenue, the advocates of reform allege that the real budget of the Party should include the large amounts raised by local Parties.

These exponents of local Party rights projected a plan of federation which would give Constituency Parties an agency through which collective opinions might be expressed and organizing work done. Briefly they proposed a national Constituency Party Association governed by an annual delegate conference, and divided into nine regional divisions with perhaps quarterly meetings of constituency representatives. By such a confederation, it was hoped that delegates from Constituency Parties might at least come to the Party's Annual Conference after some preliminary discussion of the major issues, better able to compete with the large blocks of Trade Union votes.

This proposal met with hostility from the Executive, which issued a circular to all Constituency Parties strongly urging non-adherence to the projected organization, and warning that no recognition could be accorded it under the Party Constitution.[1] The Association was launched in spite of Executive opposition, and met at Hastings just before the 1933 Conference. The local Parties have a strong case for meeting in their own national conference. As one candidate has written, " as long as four or five hundred local Party units are free to fling into the Party Conference a host of commonplace expressions of opinions and a medley of new, half-baked ideas, the influence of the political section of the Party will remain small."[2] The remedy, he suggests, is to organize the Constituency Parties into an integral section of the Party, with a real sense of unity and purpose.

Since the formation of the unofficial Constituency Party Association, the local Parties have enjoyed increasing influence at the Annual Conference. Some concession was gained at the 1933 Conference, when Regional (chiefly County) Federations of Constituency Parties were made eligible to affiliation with the

National Party, with the same standing as Central Parties in divided Boroughs.

The action of the 1937 Conference in ratifying the Executive's proposal to increase Constituency Party representation on the Executive and to allow the Parties to choose their own committee-men may do much in relieving the " half-articulate discontent " of keen Party workers described by the Coles.[3] A fundamental reorganization of the Labour Party along constituency lines would eliminate validity from the frequent charges that Labour is a sectional or class party ; it also might release and canalize reservoirs of energy now inadequately tapped.

B. Central Labour Parties

Central Parties are formed to unify the forces of Labour in Boroughs having more than one parliamentary constituency. They help establish and co-ordinate the activities of Constituency Parties within the Boroughs, and secure the Election of Labour members to municipal Councils and to Parliament. Central Parties consist of (1) affiliated organizations, including Trade Union branches, Co-operative societies, local branches of Socialist and Professional organizations, the local Trades Councils ; (2) the Constituency Parties within the Borough ; and (3) individual members enrolled in Constituency Parties.

Trades Councils, which are local federations of Trade Unions and Trade Union branches, sometimes act as Central Labour Parties in addition to their industrial functions, especially in small Boroughs with only one parliamentary division. In other cases, Central Parties act on industrial matters where no Trades Council exists. There are numerous cases where the political and the industrial functions are performed by separate sections within a combined " Trades and Labour Council " or " Trades Council and Labour Party ". Only a few are Central Parties, however. The remainder are in single constituency Boroughs and in County constituencies.

Even where a separate Central Party and Trades Council exists, the line between their respective jurisdictions is often indistinct. Primarily, however, Trades Councils are concerned with such local industrial problems as raising emergency funds for Trade Unions in distress, promoting settlements by arbitration and conciliation, and deciding demarcation disputes between Trade Unions.

Central Parties are financed by organizational affiliation fees, which are usually based on a certain rate per member per year. The Leeds Labour Party collects sixpence per affiliated member ; in Birmingham the rate is fourpence ; and the London Labour Party has a twopenny rate. A few Central Parties require a similar fee from Constituency Parties, but most require none ; nearly all distribute a proportion of centrally-collected funds to the constituencies. Campaign funds for both General and local Elections are commonly raised by Central Parties and allocated to Constituency or Ward Parties. The total budgets of Central Parties naturally vary with the size of the districts which they serve ; on the whole they raise and spend rather small amounts. For example, in 1934-5, London had a budget of £2,593 ; for 1934 Manchester £554, and Birmingham £1,187.⁴ All Central Parties except London pay an affiliation fee of £4 10s. to the National Party, and all are required to contribute to the by-election insurance fund.

The organization of the Central Party is modelled closely on that of the National Party. In place of the Annual Conference, there is a General Committee, composed of delegates from affiliated organizations. This Committee elects the Party officers and Executive Committee. It is the practice of Central Parties to divide seats on their Executives proportionately between the affiliated groups, generally giving the largest share of representation to the Trade Unions, and the second largest to Constituency Parties. Birmingham is an exception in giving Constituency Parties a majority. Representatives of the Co-operative societies are given a prominent place on Executive Committees of the more important Central Parties, and Trades Councils, if organized separately, also are granted Executive representation.

Central Parties in divided Boroughs are empowered to co-operate with Constituency Parties in the selection of candidates. If its Executive Committee has a case against the Constituency Party's selection procedure or against the prospective candidate chosen, it may report to the National Executive and recommend that endorsement be withheld. The decision to contest wards in municipal elections is made by the Central Party Executive in consultation with the Constituency

Party concerned. The Executive often invites nominations from affiliated organizations, and usually either
it or a conference or delegate meeting of the General
Committee has the power of endorsing candidates
selected by the ward organizations. General municipal
electoral policy and programme are decided by the
Central Party Executive ; provision is usually made
for Labour members of Borough Councils to report
their activities to the Central Party.

A number of useful Party services are provided
centrally by Borough Parties ; political demonstrations
and rallies are organized, local publications are issued
or supervised, Constituency Parties are assisted in
organizational problems, special campaigns are conducted, and certain propaganda work is done. In
1937, there were fifty-three Central Labour Parties in
England, Scotland and Wales, including those of the
divided Metropolitan Boroughs of London; seventeen
of them were combination " Trades Councils and
Labour Parties " or " Trades and Labour Councils ".
In addition, several Constituency Parties in double-
membered and single-membered Boroughs serve also
as Central Parties.

C. Constituency Labour Parties

Constituency Parties are charged with a greater
measure of responsibility than any of the other local
Parties. It is this unit of the Party organization which
chooses the parliamentary candidate, conducts the
campaign for Election, often guarantees the Election
expenses, and maintains the Party's essential ward and

polling district machinery in working order. Each Constituency organization also keeps up the interest of Party workers through Labour social clubs, local branches of the League of Youth, women's sections, and a host of Party social activities. A continual barrage of Party propaganda and organizational improvement is maintained by sponsoring political speakers, demonstrations, conferences with Party regional organizers, study courses, and membership drives.

A General or Management Committee, comparable to the National Party's Conference, is usually in full authority, but its decisions are subject to review by the National Executive and, ultimately, by the Annual Conference. This General Committee is a delegate body, composed of representatives of the various sections of the Party and affiliated organizations. It meets regularly, but the frequency of its meetings varies in different constituencies.

Party officers and the Executive Committee are elected by and are responsible to the General Committee. At the Executive Committee's regular meetings, Party business is reviewed, reports from wards and sections are received, and plans of development decided upon. A single Chairman presides over both the General and Executive Committees.

The Secretary is the key person in the Constituency Party. Of his numerous duties the more important include the keeping of Party records, preparation of agenda for both the Executive and the General Committees, consultation with Party and sectional officers, and general supervision over the various agencies of the Constituency Party. He often acts also as Election Agent, a statutory officer appointed by the parliamentary candidate, and in such cases it is even more essential that he possess a great amount of tact and ability to lead, for upon this important officer falls the task of marshalling the forces of the Party into fighting formation at Election times.

The Labour Party advises that the best Agents are those who can get others to work for the Party and confine themselves to planning, organizing, and directing the individual efforts of others. Upon the Agent falls the responsibility for handling all Election expenditures and for meeting the numerous legal requirements of British electoral law. The Labour Party has recognized the importance of having a full-time Agent in every constituency and has offered certain financial assistance to Constituency Parties which undertake to support one. Forty-nine Divisional Parties received grants-in-aid from the National Party for Agent's salaries during 1937.

In constituencies contested on the financial responsibility of Trade Unions, the Agent's salary usually is provided by the sponsoring Union, but actually less than one-half of the constituencies with Trade Union candidates have regular Agents. In 1935, fifty-five of the constituencies contested by Trade Unionists had Agents prior to the Election campaign ; seventy-four did not. Many of the latter were " safe " seats held by miners and others, sometimes uncontested.

If a constituency chooses a candidate of the Co-operative Party, a grant is made by the Co-operative

Party for the Constituency Agent's salary. Nine Agents were paid through such subventions in 1937. In the London area south of the Thames, the Royal Arsenal Co-operative Society, which is affiliated with both the Labour Party and the Co-operative Party, grants £40 per year to all Constituency Labour Parties which employ full-time Agents on their own responsibility. In spite of all assistance, however, less than 150 Constituency Parties are able to employ full-time Agents. A few constituencies have part-time Agents.

Selection of the parliamentary candidate is made by the General Committee of the Constituency Party. In performing this important function, the Committee is restricted by National Party constitutional provisions which require the candidate to be an individual member of the Labour Party and, if eligible, a Trade Unionist, he must agree to accept the programme, constitution, and policy of the Party, and the Standing Orders of the Parliamentary Party. A financial agreement setting forth the obligations of each is signed by the candidate or sponsoring organization and the Constituency Party.

In the interests of democracy, it may be well to retain the power of selecting parliamentary candidates in the hands of the Constituency Parties. The danger is, of course, that Party candidates are selected for such obvious considerations as the platform manner or the financial backing of the candidate, overlooking the essential qualities of leadership needed by the Party in the House of Commons. The panel maintained by the Central Office is little used in the more desirable constituencies, for they are assiduously cultivated by

Trade Unionists and by those rare specimens, prospective Labour candidates with personal fortunes. Although money probably is less important in the selection of a Labour candidate than in choosing a Liberal or a Conservative, it is a factor which is considered. Labour's rather unfortunate position in the present House of Commons, with overloaded back benches full of Labourites in their declining years and a real scarcity of the young and the able, may lead to the further extension of the National Executive's powers over endorsements. A recent proposal calls for the establishment of a central selection board to narrow down the panel of available candidates ; Constituency Parties would retain the right to make the final selection from the list of those approved centrally by the board.

Neither has the Labour Party solved the knotty problem of securing the election of front benchers as by-election candidates. Labour won sixteen by-elections between 1931 and 1935, but only in three cases (Henderson, Greenwood, and Addison) were former Cabinet Ministers chosen, although many were available and needed to bolster up the weak Labour group in the House. The same tendency for Constituency Parties to overlook national figures who are badly needed on the Labour front bench is evident since the 1935 Election. Of the first thirty-seven by-election candidates, only Wedgwood Benn and Philip Noel-Baker were political leaders of national prominence. The Conservatives in 1906 were in a position somewhat similar to that of Labour in 1931, but before the first 1910 Election many deposed Tory leaders had been returned to the House.

D. CONSTITUENCY FINANCES

The constituencies contested on the financial responsibility of Trade Unions or the Co-operative Party are quite adequately financed from centrally collected funds, but these account for little more than one-fourth of the constituencies usually contested by the Labour Party. This leaves the bulk of the parliamentary divisions to local financing ; most of these are " marginal " constituencies, either never won by Labour or won only at Elections in which the Party did exceedingly well. Financial responsibility for candidatures in the last two Elections may be shown as follows :

Sponsoring Groups	1935	1931
Local Labour Parties	400	320
Trade Unions	128	129
Co-operative Party	21	15
Scottish Socialist Party	4	—

It is considered desirable that all local Parties, for their own protection and independence, should retain some money-raising ability in order not to become completely dependent on choosing as a candidate a Trade Unionist, Co-operator, or individual who has large resources at his command. Recently the Executive and Conference have given this subject much consideration and under the decision of the 1933 Conference a contract form is now provided which limits contributions of a sponsoring organization to eighty per cent. of Election expenses, and for organizational and registration expenses to £150 per year in a Borough constituency or £200 in a County constituency. This restriction is one of the outstanding points of controversy between the Labour Party and the Co-operative Party.

The problem of obtaining and keeping membership is fundamental, both financially and organizationally, to the Constituency Party. Individual membership fees generally vary in size within each Party according to ability to pay and interest ; the penny per week contribution is becoming the most common throughout the country, although few Parties obtain a yearly average subscription of more than two shillings and sixpence. Constituency Parties employ two chief methods of increasing membership.[5] The most common is the house-to-house canvass of an area during a special membership campaign, making use of the canvass records from recent Elections and making a special effort to get all who voted Labour to join the Party. A second method, the " chain " system, involves the listing by Party members of persons known to be in sympathy with Labour ; they are invited by letter to join, and a canvasser calls at an appointed time ; if they join, they are in turn asked to list friends who might be favourably disposed toward the Party. In the operation of both schemes, an effort is made to obtain information about the persons canvassed and to approach them as Trade Unionists or Co-operators, as the case may be.

Membership is conserved chiefly through the activities of the Party collectors who make the rounds collecting weekly, monthly, or quarterly subscriptions. Each collector may make ten, twenty, thirty, or more calls a week, usually in his own neighbourhood.[6] Party fees are collected and receipted on the official membership cards provided by the Head Office for fourpence half-penny each, which is the national affiliation fee. Not only does the collector gather fees, but he also delivers notices of ward and Party activities, propaganda leaflets, announcements of public meetings and socials, copies of the local Party's journal or the *Citizen*, and a word or two of gossip on the Party. It is most essential that the collectors should do their work regularly and efficiently. Some Parties find that this task can be performed satisfactorily with voluntary help, but a number have resorted to the practice of paying a bonus of ten to twenty-five per cent. to collectors. This practice appears entirely out of harmony with the general spirit of voluntary work of which so much is done in the Labour Party. Although there may be some loss in morale, many Party Agents regard it as necessary after their membership increases beyond 2,000.

Most Constituency Parties receive a portion of their funds from local branches of Trade Unions, this being paid as affiliation fees by local Union branches for the Trade Unionists residing in the parliamentary division, or allocated by a Borough Labour Party from a centrally collected fund. An increasing number of Co-operative societies are paying Co-operators' affiliation fees to local Labour Parties. Although these two sources are of importance to local Parties, nevertheless, such affiliated members often feel no further obligation to the Party. Therefore, most Parties make strenuous attempts to get Trade Unionists and Co-operators to become active as well as affiliated members.

E. Propaganda Work in the Constituencies

In propaganda work, local Parties are constantly urged by the Head Office to make periodical examinations of the nature of the constituency's population, to study it by occupational and other social groups, and to employ what Sidney Webb has termed " stratified electioneering ".[7] This involves making a specialized appeal to various sections of voters, discovered by a study of census returns on occupations, and by examination of membership rolls of Trade Unions, Co-operatives, Churches, and other groups.

Above all other factors, the real source of strength of the Labour Party is the day to day work of its convinced partisans who sacrifice their time and money for the " cause ". The other Parties have attempted to imitate both by levying a small membership fee and by enlisting voluntary workers, but neither the Liberals nor the Conservatives have enjoyed much success. Indeed, one Conservative has ascribed much of Labour's success to its appeal, " . . . embodied in the actual and continual sacrifice by thousands of party workers of the scanty leisure which the conditions of their work allows them ! "[8]

The work is carried on in the constituencies throughout the year. Speakers are booked by the Party for both ward and constituency public meetings ; during special campaigns and in the summer months open air street meetings are arranged. The Head Office and sometimes the Central Parties issue monthly propaganda posters which are used widely. A few Constituency Parties have issued their own newspapers or magazines, containing news of the social and political activities of the Party, and occasional articles on Labour policy.

A much larger number, however, finding themselves unable to finance an individual organ, contract for the *Citizen*, a monthly four-page newspaper issued at a very low cost by the Co-operative Press, Ltd. The two outside pages are devoted to local constituency news by local correspondents ; the inner pages contain standard national news written from the Co-operative point of view. The paper was used by more than sixty constituencies, and its average circulation was 700,000 during 1935 ; at General Election time, its circulation reached 2,520,000.[9] Local Parties were charged £12 10s. for 10,000 copies each month, part of which cost may easily be met from local advertising. The *Citizen* is chiefly circulated in England, especially around London where both the London Co-operative Society and the Royal Arsenal Co-operative Society have subsidized it heavily. Both independent Party organs and the *Citizen* are distributed to Party members and sympathizers by voluntary Party workers and by the regular Party collectors. Some local Party papers are sold for one penny, when it can be obtained, but papers usually are left whether paid for or not.

Local Parties rely very largely on the Head Office

for printed propaganda, for it issues a great volume of leaflets, pamphlets, and posters. These are sold to local Parties at cost ; the leaflets are distributed free in the constituencies, but pamphlets are sold. At every Labour meeting and in every Party committee room Party literature is on sale.

The problem of providing books in sufficient quantities for reading and study by Party members is not yet satisfactorily solved. The Fabian Society has for years loaned large boxes of books on social and economic subjects to Trade Unions, Co-operatives, and local Parties, but the number of local Parties taking advantage of this service is relatively small.[10] The great advance in British public libraries has remedied the situation considerably. The Left Book Club, organized in early 1936, has succeeded in bringing at low cost many outstanding books to its 50,000 subscribers, most of whom must be of Labour sympathies.

F. WARD PARTIES, WOMEN'S SECTIONS, AND YOUTH GROUPS

Much of the urban Constituency Party work is done through ward Committees or Associations. The individual membership of the Party is divided by wards, and many members make their chief contributions to the Party through ward organizations. The more active ward Associations meet regularly, usually once a month, on a quasi-social basis with a measure of political propaganda mixed in. Committee rooms for wards are often rented by the Party, and occasionally are actually owned by it. It is common practice in

Constituency Parties to allocate the responsibility for membership fee collections to the ward Committee.

The ward Secretary is the chief officer, and keeps the ward Association in touch with the Constituency Party. Sub-committees of the ward group generally exist in each of the polling districts. This precinct organization is the basic cell of the Party machinery. It arranges for street captains and canvass leaders, and plans the general scheme of the Party's approach to the particular neighbourhood. Commonly financial agreements are made by the Constituency Party whereby a certain percentage of money collected by the ward organization for individual memberships is returned for ward purposes.

In County or rural areas, the Village or Town Labour Party is the organizational unit of the Constituency Party instead of the ward, but its problems and organizations are similar to those of the ward. Greater difficulty is encountered by partisans in rural districts because of the scattered membership and the hesitancy of the people to identify themselves with a movement disapproved of by their employers or landowners. Polling district organization and work in rural areas are much the same as in Boroughs although it is frequently necessary to carry on Party activities more secretly.

Under the National Party Constitution, women members of the Party are enrolled in both the regular ward organizations and in women's sections, which may be formed by wards or districts. Women's sections have proven a very effective recruiting agency for the Party, and often raise considerable amounts of money through bazaars and various kinds of socials. These women's groups constitute a tremendous source of strength for the Labour Party, for they harness the energy of many who can render daytime service during special and Election campaigns. Meetings are held in the afternoons, as often as once a week, and over a cup of tea the women chat about community affairs, discuss Party socials and other activities, and listen to a speaker on some political subject. Women's sections are represented on Constituency Party Executive Committees, and many send delegates to the National Conference of Labour Women.

The nature and extent of activities carried on by Labour women's groups may be judged from a review of their work during 1934 in Bristol East, one of the most carefully organized Labour constituencies.[11]   A regular Wednesday afternoon " old time learners' dance class " netted a profit which was used for propaganda among women. A yearly women's rally and six monthly rallies were occasions for political speakers. The Bristol East women held a Party supper, a garden party, and a jumble sale ; all yielded profits which enriched the local Party treasury.

Party " bazaars " have come to form a major function of many local Party women's groups. The backbone of the sale is the " work stall ", where the women sell articles and garments made by themselves. In addition, stalls for the sale of refreshments, " junk ", books, novelties, and other commodities usually are operated. During 1933 the Reading Constituency

Party raised £558 from bazaars ; in 1934 it cleared about £300 from the same source.[12] Other Parties have done nearly as well, and bazaar income now constitutes an important part of local Party funds. The social intercourse which Party sales, whist drives, dances, and entertainments provide is extremely important to working class housewives.

Although severely shaken by the reorganization of 1936, the League of Youth still has branches in a majority of constituencies. Membership is open to young people from sixteen to twenty-one years of age ; and the League's object is to foster interest in Party work through a range of social, forensic, dramatic, and athletic activities. Some Constituency Parties get a large amount of valuable service from their youth groups, but there is a high record of mortality among the League branches, especially in the rural areas. According to a recent social study of the unemployed, the League of Youth branches are drawing many youngsters from Church circles.[13]

The local branches and organizations of the Labour Party play a very important role in the social life of most industrial communities. A recent social investigation of the Liverpool area revealed that the Labour Party maintained clubs in nearly every ward in the city.[14] The survey also disclosed forty-six Conservative Clubs in the region, many of them for working men. This may help to explain the surprising strength of the Tories in the industrial port. Some of the 109 political clubs in London are Labour Clubs, but the political tests of membership often are enforced

laxly, if at all.[15]   The women's sections of the local
Parties offer the most in social outlets ; they provide
for many women the contacts and fellowship which
their husbands receive in their Trade Unions and Clubs.

G.   Party Organization in London

The magnitude of the area and the complexity of
local governmental jurisdictions make the problem of
the Party organization in London a peculiarly different
one.   Party work in the Administrative County of
London (governed by the London County Council),
is headed by the London Labour Party.   Central
Parties exist in nineteen of the twenty-eight London
Metropolitan Boroughs which have more than one
parliamentary constituency.   In addition, every one
of the sixty-two constituencies inside the County
(except the two in the City of London) have
Constituency Labour Parties.

Among the functions of the London Labour Party
are the general conduct of Party business concerning
the London County Council, the supervision of
organizational work in the area, the planning of central
demonstrations and propaganda efforts, the publication
of a monthly newspaper, *The London News*, and the
organization of special campaigns.[16]   The London
Party has done a good deal in the collection of data on
various municipal problems, has called a number of
conferences of Labour Councillors and Aldermen, and
has been very aggressive about advising the Labour
groups on Borough Councils on the conduct of their
Party caucuses.   Unquestionably, much of the credit

for the excellent showing made by Labour in London during recent years is due to the efficient work of the London Party's Secretary, Mr Herbert Morrison, now Leader of the London County Council.

Inevitably the Borough Parties in London are confined to rather minor matters because of the strength of the central London Party. In practice they are limited to the determination of policy and endorsement of candidates for Borough Council elections, and to acting as Trades Councils, for most of these Parties are combined industrial-political Trades Council and Labour Parties. A few years ago the London Party made a strong drive for the abolition of the Borough Parties and the substitution of standing joint committees to conduct the small business of each Borough as a whole, financed by equal contributions of the Constituency Parties within the Borough. This proposal met strong opposition at the time and was dropped, but some simplification of the Party organization in London probably could be made without weakening the position of the Party and with a real saving to affiliated organizations.

In 1920 the National Executive rejected a proposal to amalgamate the London Labour Party and the London Trades Council ; it was held that union would yield advantages to neither, nor could any real savings be made by maintaining a joint office.[17]

The Constituency Parties in the London area operate in much the same way as in the provincial cities, except that they are, in general, better organized and thereby able to produce better results at the polls.

CHAPTER FIVE

REFERENCES

1 *Daily Herald*, September 27th, 1933.

2 *Labour Candidate*, September 1932.

3 G. D. H. and M. I. Cole, *A Guide to Modern Politics* (London, 1934), p. 11.

4 *The Work of the London Labour Party*, 1934-5, p. 29. *Manchester Borough Labour Party Annual Report, Balance Sheet and Directory, 1934-5*, p. 28. *Birmingham Trades Council, Borough Labour Party Annual Report and Year Book, 1934-5*, p. 73.

5 *Party Organization*, issued by the Labour Party (London, 1933, 4th edition), pp. 33-5.

6 The Southampton Party collectors vary from 2 to 110 visits ; those making the most calls usually do the best job. *Labour Organizer*, No. 166 (April 1935), pp. 71-2, 75.

7 *The Conduct of Elections*, issued by the Labour Party (London, 1931), p. 3 ; G. R. Shepherd, " Candidates and the Labour Resurgence," *Labour Candidate*, August-September 1933, p. 1.

8 E. Thomas Cook, " The Electors Demand a Policy," *Conservatism and the Future* (London, 1935), p. 312.

9 *The Report of the Central Board to the 68th Annual Congress of the Co-operative Union, Newcastle-upon-Tyne, 1936*, p. 175.

10 It was reported as 18 in 1931 ; 25 in 1932 ; 15 in 1933 ; 16 in 1934 ; and 13 in 1935. *Fifty-second Annual Report on the Work of the Fabian Society* (London, 1936).

11 Bristol East Divisional Labour Party, *Seventeenth Annual Report, Statement of Accounts and Balance Sheet* (February 28th, 1935), p. 1.

[12] *Labour Organizer*, No. 153 (March 1934), p. 50 ; *Ibid.*, No. 165 (March 1935), p. 46.

[13] E. Wight Bakke, *The Unemployed Man : A Social Study* (London, 1933), p. 217.

[14] D. Caradog Jones, *The Social Survey of Merseyside*, Vol. iii (London, 1934), p. 308.

[15] *The New Survey of London Life and Labour*, Vol. ix (London, 1934), pp. 31-2.

[16] *Labour Party Organization in London*, issued by the London Labour Party, 1930, p. 4.

[17] *Short History of the London Trades Council* (London, 1935), pp. 64-5.

THE CO-OPERATIVE PARTY

A. EARLY RELATIONSHIP WITH THE LABOUR PARTY

THE original plan of a " Federal Alliance " of working class organizations to form one political movement included the participation of the Co-operative societies. But the Co-operatives sent no delegates to the Conference of 1900 at which the Labour Representation Committee was organized, choosing rather to maintain their traditional neutrality in politics. When, however, the Co-operative trading enterprise suffered from governmental discriminations during the World War, the prejudices of the Movement against political action were swept away by the indignation of the delegates to the Co-operative Congress of 1917, who decided to establish the Co-operative Party as a separate political Party.[1] The Party was organized at a special Conference in London later in the same year ; its objects and programme were strikingly similar to those of the Labour Party at that time.

From the beginning there has been a close relationship between the Co-operative Party and the Labour Party. Negotiations for an agreement were started in 1919, and the Co-operative Party, after consultation with representatives of the Labour Party and the Trades

Union Congress, drafted a proposed political alliance of the three bodies, which would have involved the establishment of a joint committee equally representing the trinity, with power to make declarations on common policy, endorse parliamentary candidates, secure concerted action in the constituencies, and to arbitrate differences arising between local groups. The 1921 Co-operative Congress rejected the alliance by the close vote of 1,686,000 to 1,682,000.[2]

Without any formal agreement, however, Labour and Co-operative forces made local arrangements in the few constituencies where Co-operative candidates stood. Under such conditions one Co-operative candidate was elected in 1918, four were elected in 1922, and six were returned in 1923, of whom four served in minor capacities in the first Labour Government. Although the Co-operative Party was reduced to five seats after the 1924 Election, its close relationship with Labour in the House continued, and two Co-operative Members of Parliament became Labour junior whips. Not only were Co-operators welcomed into the Parliamentary Labour Party and given posts of responsibility there, but also their cause was supported constantly by the Labour group.

Co-operators justified this close collaboration with the Labour Movement on the grounds that the two-party system was inevitable in British politics, and that the Labour policy was in general agreement with the Co-operative aspirations toward a "Co-operative Commonwealth". Like so many things in British life, the relationship just grew, and eventually the once hesitant Co-operative Congress came to accept it.   The chief opposition rose, not from hostility to political action, for its necessity was widely admitted, but from the fear that alliance with the Labour Party would injure Co-operative business.   Therefore, the most effective argument advanced in favour of a Co-operative Labour agreement was that unofficial action had obtained results which were advantageous to Co-operative trading and that business had not decreased because of the relationship.[3]   On the initiative of the 1925 Co-operative Congress, perhaps motivated by conflicts between local Labour and local Co-operative Parties in two parliamentary constituencies, new negotiations for an agreement were opened.

B.   THE LABOUR–CO-OPERATIVE AGREEMENT OF 1927

An agreement drafted by the National Committee of the Co-operative Party and the Executive of the Labour Party was subsequently ratified, in 1927, by both the Co-operative Congress and the Labour Party Conference, and provides the basis for the present alliance of the two forces.   It creates a national joint committee, representing the Executives of the two Parties, which holds meetings and exercises powers subject to the two Executives.   The Executives exchange minutes, and may arrange joint special and election campaigns.   Locally, the agreement makes Co-operative Parties or Councils eligible for regular affiliation with Constituency Labour Parties, on the basis of mutually agreeable fees, which are subject to the approval of the National Parties.   The formation of local agreements is optional with local Co-operative and Labour Parties.

In practice, this agreement with the Labour Party has worked advantageously to both Parties. Its terms are sufficiently general to allow adjustments to particular circumstances. Many local agreements have been filed with the two National Parties, and the relationship has been harmonious except for occasional local controversies. Apart from one case in 1924, local differences have never been carried to the extent of both Parties contesting the same constituency at a General Election. Labour aid is indispensable to the Co-operative Party, and most Co-operative political leaders recognize that perhaps no Co-operative candidate could win without Labour support. Co-operators as such lack the political consciousness that is necessary to build an effective Party machine. The Co-operative Party, by assuming responsibility for an increasing number of candidates, has relieved the Labour Party of a heavy financial burden. Moreover, in some constituencies Co-operators have a better chance of winning than Labourites, because of the large number of Co-operative members in the division.

Some outspoken criticism of the Labour–Co-operative alliance has come from certain sections of the Co-operative Movement. In general, the most common complaint is that the Co-operative Party is only a " weak reflection " of the Labour Party, a condition which is allegedly inappropriate for the " largest political party in the nation ".[4] Specifically, some

Co-operators demand the termination of the agreement, and the building of a great National Party from the Co-operative Movement.   Others, taking a more realistic approach, confine their suggestions to obtaining more constituencies for Co-operative candidates, persuading Labour to adjust its policy in certain particulars, or establishing local Co-operative Parties on a firmer basis.[5]

On the other hand, the Labour Party is concerned with approaching full unity with the Co-operative Movement by urging closer alliance nationally and by increasing local affiliation and joint action.   The encouraging progress on the national front, manifested by the Co-operative Union's participation in demonstrations against unemployment cuts in 1933, appears to have been halted by the decision of the National Co-operative Authority not to join the National Council of Labour when invited in 1935.   Nevertheless, efforts of the Labour Party to secure closer co-operation will go on, for the Co-operative Movement has a huge membership and great financial resources which may yet be enlisted in the political cause of a substantially united British working class.   During the 1935 General Election campaign, the National Co-operative Authority issued a manifesto urging all Co-operative societies to unite to defeat the National Government.   This was the first occasion when an official Co-operative political appeal has been directed to all societies, irrespective of Party affiliation.

During 1936-7 special negotiations were opened between the Labour and the Co-operative Movements in an attempt to settle outstanding differences bearing on the local relationships of the Co-operative Party and the Labour Party. A satisfactory arrangement has not been reached. The main points of conflict arise over Co-operative Party ambitions to achieve full independence and strength and Labour's aspirations for discipline and unity. The chief points of contention may be summarized as follows :[6]

LABOUR POSITION	CO-OPERATIVE POSITION
Affiliation	
Local Co-operative Parties should affiliate with local Labour Parties, just as do Trade Union branches and other groups.	Local Co-operative Parties and local Labour Parties should make joint agreements for political collaboration.
Agents	
All Constituency Agents should be servants of the Labour Party, including divisions with candidates of Co-operative sponsorship.	Constituency Agents of divisions contested by Co-operative candidates should be under Co-operative Party control.
Finances	
Co-operative sponsored candidates must be subject to the same financial restrictions (imposed by the Labour Party) which apply to other Labour candidates.	Co-operative candidatures should be financed from Co-operative funds without Labour interference.
Loyalty	
All Labour – Co-operative candidates must pledge loyalty to the Labour Party.	Co-operative candidates owe primary allegiance to Co-operative Movement.

C. Structure and Record of the Co-operative Party

The Co-operative Party is organically bound to the Co-operative Union, the federation of British Co-operative societies, through the Party's National Committee, which is a committee of the Union and responsible to the Executive Committee of the Union. The National Committee is composed of representatives from each of the chief elements in the Movement, including eight members from Sectional Boards of the Co-operative Union, eight from Sectional Groups of Societies contributing to the political fund, two from the Co-operative Wholesale Society, Ltd., two from the Co-operative Joint Parliamentary Committee, and one each from a variety of Co-operative educational, trading and social organizations. A Party Executive Committee is elected by and from the National Committee.[7]

The two Committees share the responsibility for framing a statement of programme and policy in harmony with decisions of the Co-operative Congress ; and it is their duty to encourage and aid local Co-operative political endeavours, to administer the political fund, to endorse parliamentary candidates, and to prepare propaganda and educational literature on political subjects.[8] The Co-operative Party has held an Annual Conference for the past ten years, but, due to the Party's lack of autonomy, the Conference's decisions are not conclusive, for it ultimately must bow to the will of the Co-operative Union and Congress,

The Co-operative Union maintains for the Party a Head Office in London, with a small staff headed by the Party Secretary, S. F. Perry, a former Labour-Co-operative Member of Parliament. Four regional organizers work out of the Central Office ; they make the rounds of Co-operative societies and guilds, urging affiliation with the Party, and with local Parties and Political Councils, and advise on organization. Through its organizers, the Party seeks the affiliation of the various retail Co-operative societies by way of its " contracting in " plan, whereby affiliated Co-operatives pay a fee of one halfpenny per year for each of their members. The first approach of the organizer is to the board of management of the society he is encouraging to join the Party. If the board refuses to affiliate, he proceeds to form a " voluntary " local Party of members of the society who desire to take political action. From within the society the voluntary Party group then urges the case for affiliation with the Party.

After the affiliation of a society, a regular local Co-operative Party is formed, the more active members becoming an " individual members section ". The latter collects a subscription fee from its members, and generally constitutes the active portion of the local Party. Strictly speaking, the local Party is composed of representatives from the society's management and education committees, men's and women's guilds, elected society members, and others. The Central Office recommends that quarterly meetings be held, and that an executive committee conduct the day to day affairs of the Party.[9]   The number of active local Parties in the country is probably exceedingly small.[10] These Parties are financed almost entirely by contributions from their local societies.   Co-operative candidates for local offices are advanced by the local Party or Political Council in the district ; agreements are reached with the local Labour Party, and the candidates formally adopted.   Constituencies are secured for Co-operative parliamentary candidates by negotiation with Constituency Labour Parties.

The organizers also supervise the activities of federations of Co-operative Parties which are subsidized by the Party, as well as the local Party organizations in those constituencies in which there are endorsed Co-operative candidates.

The growth of the Co-operative Party is shown in the following table :[11]

Year		Affiliated Societies		Membership
1924	..	393	..	1,835,671
1925	..	447	..	2,000,644
1926	..	435	..	2,009,240
1927	..	444	..	2,376,654
1928	..	421	..	2,464,891
1929	..	427	..	2,795,490
1930	..	423	..	3,281,971
1931	..	434	..	3,522,566
1932	..	424	..	3,670,650
1933	..	462	..	4,083,531
1934	..	477	..	4,410,368
1935	..	502	..	5,100,000

The increase in affiliated membership has been steady.   The 502 Societies within the Party in 1935 represented sixty-six per cent. of the total British Co-operative membership. The fortunes of the Party at Elections appear as follows :

Co-operative Candidates :

	1918	1922	1923	1924	1929	1931	1935
Seats contested	10	11	10	10	12	15	20
Seats won	1	4	6	5	9	1	9

The National Committee was able to report to the 1935 Party Conference that 536 Co-operative-nominated persons were serving on various local authorities ; in 1936, 647 Co-operative municipal office holders were reported.

The Head Office of the Party issues considerable amounts of propaganda literature. Some of its leaflet material appears to be rather effective, but the policy pamphlets, the " Britain Reborn " series, are unimpressive and immature. Generous publicity of the Party activities is given in the numerous publications of the movement, such as the *Co-operative Review*, the *Co-operative Productive Review*, the *Co-operative Guildsman* (all monthlies), the *Co-operative News* (weekly), and the popular Sunday, *Reynold's News*. The *Citizen*, which has already been described, carries on its national pages chiefly the Co-operative Party point of view. Information for speakers is issued by the Party through *Monthly Party Notes*.

D. CO-OPERATIVE POLITICAL FINANCING

The Co-operative Party has drawn from the successful example of the Labour Party the practice of financing itself by affiliation fees. There are now more than seven million co-operators in the United Kingdom ; the Movement has enormous financial resources, and the diversion of a portion of its trading surplus for political purposes was found rather easy to accomplish. Indeed, the levy of one halfpenny per member has produced more income for the Party than it has been able to spend efficiently ; its real budget amounts to about one-third that of the National Labour Party, but its organizational and propaganda work reaches a much smaller fraction of the electorate.

The largest part of the Co-operative Party's income is derived from affiliation fees from retail Co-operative societies which choose to pay the political levy for their members ; during 1934 they paid £8,576 at the rate of one halfpenny per member ; during 1935 they paid £9,377 ; in addition, the Co-operative Wholesale Society and the Scottish Co-operative Wholesale Society contribute £1,000 and £500, respectively, each year. There are a few minor sources of income, but they are insignificant.

Although the Party does not actually handle the funds, an additional £3,000 or more is furnished by the Co-operative Union for the expenses of the Party Central Office, which is considered a department of the Union ; this sum is accepted as the contribution of the Co-operative Union to the political fund, although it may contribute additional amounts if it chooses.

The Party does not account for its Central Office expenditures of funds furnished by the Co-operative Union ; but these disbursements presumably include rent, salaries of the Secretary and Organizers, general administrative expenses, and certain literature charges. Apparently the Co-operative Union spent nearly £6,000 on the Party during 1935.[12]

Expenditures of the Party from the regular political fund include a surprising number of large items for travelling and other expenses of committees and officers, which are most generous in comparison with the frugal allowances in the Labour Party budget for more essential purposes. Grants of £50 per year are made towards Agents' salaries in constituencies where Co-operative candidates have been selected ; in addition, £90 yearly is granted to such constituencies to aid in the distribution of the *Citizen*.[13] The Party spent about £7,500 in the General Election campaign of 1935. Two-thirds of Election expenses are furnished by the national Co-operative Party for its officially sponsored candidates.[14] The remainder of the Party's expenses are for propaganda, literature, conferences, demonstrations, grants to local groups, and sundries. The normal expenditures are much below the usual income, and a reserve of more than £15,000 had been accumulated by the beginning of 1935[15] ; one year later it was £12,000.

A comparison of the national financing of the Labour Party and that of the Co-operative Party reveals a great contrast ; the former, with very large obligations, manages to maintain its position as a major political party on modest resources ; the latter is plentifully supplied with funds, which it spends freely on essentials and otherwise. Admittedly, the job of making

Co-operators politically conscious is more difficult and costly than getting Trade Unionists and others to participate in Labour politics. But even allowing for this, it is doubtful if the Co-operative Movement is getting its money's worth out of the sums allocated for political purposes.

E. Political Activities of the London Co-operative Society

The political work of the London Co-operative Society indicates the general direction of the activities of larger retail Societies in the field of politics. This Society in 1936 had 583,380 members and is the largest of all the British Co-operatives ; its trade for the year 1935 amounted to more than £12,000,000 ; it is engaged in the retailing of nearly every article for domestic use, in light manufacturing and farming, and in providing a great variety of services to its members. The London Society operates in the east, north, and west areas of London and the suburbs, chiefly north of the Thames.

The Society's membership elects a Political Committee of fifteen and charges it with the conduct of all political activities and the administration of the political fund, to which two and one-half per cent. of the trading surplus is appropriated. For the year 1934-5, the Political Committee was allocated £13,734.[16] Like the national Co-operative Party, the Society has an Annual Conference with little power ; its resolutions are in terms such as " urge the necessity ", " is of the opinion ", " regrets ", " condemns ", " protests ",

" resents ", and " recommends " ; the Conference is no more than an arena for the expression of aspirations and the discussion of local problems. The Political Committee, acting through its permanent Secretary and a full-time Organizer, organizes local Political Councils which are made up of individual members and are usually affiliated as a group with local Labour Parties. There were seventy-eight Political Councils with 3,500 to 4,000 individual members in January 1936.

Winter " concert meetings " are the chief activity of the Councils. These are arranged centrally in the Committee's office ; the programme usually consists of a musical or vaudeville programme given by professional entertainers ; halfway through, one or two political speeches are delivered by a Co-operative-Labour candidate for Parliament or a municipal office. The attendance at the 119 concert meetings arranged for 1934-5 was reported to average about 400 per event ; ninety-one meetings were planned for the season 1935-6. Often the audiences are made up chiefly of women and children, who obviously come for entertainment rather than for the political address. In the arrangement of the meetings, almost nothing is left to local discretion ; both speakers and artists are booked and paid centrally, and even details of local hall and printing arrangements must be reported to, and paid for, by the Head Office.

Two series of regional conferences are called annually by the Political Committee, and are reasonably well attended. For 1935, the topics were " The Place of

Co-operation in the Socialist State ", and " Collective Security ".[17] The Committee sponsors week-end schools both at Easter and in the autumn for the consideration of political questions, and takes part in some of the demonstrations of the Labour Party and other groups. About £1,000 yearly is spent in subsidizing the London distribution of the *Citizen*, the Co-operative-produced combination local-national newspaper. Thirty-three constituencies have taken advantage of the London Society's generous offer of 10,000 copies for £2 monthly. The Society places advertising in the *Citizen*, so the amount of the Political Committee's subsidy is about £6 per 10,000 monthly.

The Political Committee issues *Co-operative Politics*, a monthly four-page propaganda organ, usually containing an article or two on Party or national affairs. The sheet lacks substance and imagination. The Political Committee also contributes financially to the *Wheatsheaf* the monthly organ of the Society, which carries announcements of the various Political Councils, as well as general Society news.

Co-operators become candidates for municipal and parliamentary seats through the machinery of the local Labour Parties. Their names are proposed to Constituency Labour Parties by the Political Council or Councils in the division. If approved Co-operators are chosen, the Political Committee makes a grant toward election expenses, the amount varying according to the office sought. About £5 is contributed to each candidate for Metropolitan Borough Councils ;

a larger amount is granted to candidates for the London County Council. The national Co-operative Party pays the expenses of Co-operative parliamentary candidates. To qualify for the financial support of the London Society, a person must have made total purchases at the Society's stores amounting to £30 during the past year.

London Political Councils meet each fortnight or month. Federations of Political Councils exist in five areas to co-ordinate Council work and to arrange area conferences. The Council meetings very frequently are addressed by Labour Party members and candidates. Activities of the local Councils are financed by grants from the central Committee for such purposes as rent, postage, and the like ; also by a subscription fee paid by individual members of (usually) sixpence yearly.

Although its local Political Councils are affiliated with local Labour Parties, the Political Committee has consistently declined to affiliate centrally with the London Labour Party. It refused to discuss the subject in 1933, but agreed to meet a Labour delegation to confer on the affiliation of Political Councils with local Labour Parties. After the consultation, the Political Committee announced its decision that the existing relationship must remain, holding that any change might be " detrimental to national development ".[18] One London Society politician once expressed it a little more concretely, declaring : "We're going to spend our own money, not hand it over to the Labour Party."

Seven of the Co-operative Party's twenty candidates

in the 1935 General Election were for constituencies in the London Co-operative Society's area ; five were successful. London Co-operative Political Councils proposed eighty-five candidates for the municipal elections of November 1934, and fifty-nine were successful.[19] The London Co-operative Society Political Committee paid £970 in affiliation fees to the Co-operative Party for the year 1934-5.

F. POLITICAL ACTIVITIES OF THE ROYAL ARSENAL CO-OPERATIVE SOCIETY

The second leading London Co-operative, the Royal Arsenal Co-operative Society, has also participated a great deal in politics, but its approach is very different from that of the London Society. The Royal Arsenal serves a membership of about 320,000 and carries on an annual trade of £8,000,000 ; it has entered an even greater range of enterprises than its colleague across the Thames. The area served by the Royal Arsenal is London and suburbs south of the river, a region more solidly working class in composition than that covered by the London Society.

The Political Purposes Committee of the Society directs all political activities and administers the political fund to which sixpence annually is allocated from general funds for every member of the Society, except for those who notify the Society of their objections to political activity. About 2,000 per year request to " contract out ".

The Committee consists of twelve members, of whom eight are elected by the members, two are appointed by the General (Management) Committee, and two by the Educational Committee. Grants to the political fund for 1934-5 totalled £7,468.[20] The chief task of the Committee is the allocation of this fund to the various agencies which the Society sees fit to support.

Directly after the Society's decision to enter politics in May 1921, application was made to the Labour Party for affiliation. The Society was admitted to the Labour Party nationally, and it and its guilds (social-educational groups) joined also the London Labour Party and all the Borough, Constituency, and local Labour Parties in its area ; these connections have been maintained constantly since that time. Practically the whole of its political funds is used to pay affiliation fees and to make grants to Labour Parties.

The Society paid £534 in national affiliation fees to the Labour Party in 1933 and 1934, and £600 in 1935. The sum of £400 annually is paid to the London Labour Party. Yielding to pressure from within the Society, the Political Purposes Committee in 1930 affiliated also with the Co-operative Party, to which it pays £400 per year. In support of the local Labour Parties in its area, with which the Society is most concerned, annual grants of £40 are made to all Constituency Parties employing full-time Agents, and £600 is distributed among all Constituency Labour Parties in proportion to the Society's membership in each parliamentary division. In addition, one-third of the whole political fund is allocated in the same proportion to local Labour Parties. This amounted to £2,313 in 1933 and about £2,500 in 1934.[21] Special grants are made to Labour Parties, local and national, for election purposes ; £50 was donated in 1934 to the London County Council Election fund, and £100 to the 1935 Labour General Election fund. Smaller grants are made for Borough Council and Urban District Council elections. A subsidy is allowed for the distribution of the *Citizen* in eleven constituencies within the Society's area ; the monthly issue of 10,000 copies is made available to Constituency Labour Parties for the sum of £3.

Unlike the London Society and the Co-operative Party, the Royal Arsenal spends a comparatively small amount for office and administrative expenses ; this charge averages between £1,000 and £1,500 yearly. The Political Purposes Committee is concerned chiefly with the proper spending of its political fund through the existing Labour Party organization, and with securing adequate representation of Co-operative interests on local authorities and in Parliament. By virtue of its affiliation fees and grants, the Society receives representation on the governing committees of the twenty-eight Labour Parties with which it is connected, usually by five members on the General (Management) Committee and two on the Executive Committee. These Co-operative representatives in the various Labour Parties meet quarterly to discuss Labour and Co-operative problems, and delegates from them keep in touch with the Political Purposes Committee of the Society.

The proposing of Co-operators for local public offices is done in the local Labour Parties through

Co-operative General or Executive Committee-men. Special campaign grants are made in all cases where panel Co-operators are adopted as candidates. Co-operators must have purchased £40 in goods from the Society in the past year ; the same requirement is enforced for Society offices and those who serve as Co-operative representatives on local Parties.

If the success of its participation in politics may be measured by the number of public offices held, then the Royal Arsenal has achieved a most satisfactory record and its scheme of working through the Labour Party is vindicated. In January 1935 the Secretary of the Committee was able to report the status of his Co-operative's representation in municipal government as follows :[22]

	On Panel	Adopted by Labour Parties	Elected
London County Council	17	14	12
Borough Councils	140	108	86
Urban District Councils	20	18	6

Since 1930, when the Royal Arsenal Society joined the Co-operative Party, its parliamentary candidatures have been handled through and financed by the Co-operative Party. In the 1935 General Elections W. H. Green, Secretary of the Political Purposes Committee, secured election to Parliament ; a second Royal Arsenal candidate was defeated by a narrow margin. Likewise, this Society has been prominently represented in the higher councils of the Labour Party ; three representatives serve on the London Labour Party Executive Committee, and a Royal Arsenalite

has been elected to the National Party Executive for
years.   A former (1935-6) National Chairman of the
Labour Party, Mrs J. L. Adamson, although holding
that post as representative of a local Party, was also a
member of the Royal Arsenal Political Purposes
Committee.

The central idea behind the participation of the
Royal Arsenal Society in Labour politics is that there
is no room for a competing Co-operative Party and
that a united working class within the Labour Party is
the surest bulwark in defence of democratic institutions.
Although it joined the Co-operative Party to quiet
internal agitation, perhaps to keep competing Co-
operative Political Councils out of its area, and to
obtain financing for its parliamentary candidates,
Royal Arsenal's political policy would appear directed
toward the eventual union of the Co-operative Party
with the Labour Party.

G.   THE STAKE OF BRITISH CO-OPERATIVES IN POLITICS

Holyoake and other pioneers of the British Co-
operative Movement warned their followers that when
" politicians attack Co-operation, co-operators must
become politicians."[23]   The entry of the Co-operatives
into politics did come as a result of alleged political
attacks during the war.   Basically, the Co-operative
Party sprang from the economic interests of Co-operation, and its chief end in politics to-day is to defend
Co-operative trading interests.   Co-operative Members
of Parliament are concerned with minor adjustments
in legislation likely to affect the vast businesses of the

9

Co-operative societies. Their success in this role on one hand, and the renewed attacks on the Movement by private traders on the other, has forced the Co-operatives farther and farther into political action.

The recent intensification of legislative attacks on Co-operatives probably is due in part to the participation of the Movement in politics. The Finance Act of 1933 brought Co-operative's trading surplus under the income tax ; Co-operative members on municipal Councils were prevented from voting on contracts with the society to which they belong. Co-operative interests have suffered from the operation of the National Government's marketing schemes, which they allege tend to stabilize existing " capitalist agencies " and to prevent Co-operatives from expanding at the expense of their existing competitors.

Theoretically, the Co-operative Party looks to the establishment of a " Co-operative Commonwealth ", with the socialist features of " production for use " and " common ownership ". There appear to be no serious objections to the general outline of the Labour programme, but Co-operators are much concerned to see that, in the socialist state of the future, the Co-operatives are given control of distribution and that the Movement shall be permitted to buy freely in the world market. Few Labour leaders are irreparably wedded to the idea of free trade, but rather full *laissez-faire* is demanded by Co-operative spokesmen.

Drawn into political action by wartime governmental discrimination, British Co-operatives projected a new Party and cautiously fell into a working agreement with the Labour Party. This approach was the way of compromise : the feet of the Co-operative giant slid into the pond of Labour politics, but the body remains sprawled on the bank, undecided whether to risk following the feet, or to withdraw them and let them dry in the possibly arid atmosphere of non-partisanship. The giant is confused further by the angry barking of capitalist bulldogs on the bank and by the inviting croakings of socialist bullfrogs in the pool.

A delegate at the 1937 Co-operative Congress, W. McLaine, of the London Society, stated the dilemma of Co-operative politics with humour and incisiveness :[24]

The fact is that the Co-operative Party is a sham. The Movement has never really taken politics seriously. The trading side of the Movement is only too anxious to say, " We will give you some money, but do not let anybody know you are related to us." (Laughter.) " If you are poor—you cannot do your political work without money—more's the pity, or we would let you do it." (Laughter.) " We will give you some of our profits, but when we are passing you in the street, please do not let anybody know you know us." (Laughter.)

The Party has failed to capture the imagination of the Movement. Until it captures the imagination of the Movement it cannot capture the imagination of the crowd outside. Does anybody doubt that the Party has failed to capture the imagination of the Movement ? Does anyone suggest for a single solitary moment that these 5,000,000 politically conscious and determined co-operators are doing all I mentioned ? Well, we know they are not. . . .

The clear-cut alternatives before the British Co-operative Movement would seem to have been two : either the Co-operatives should have remained safely neutral, or they should have entered whole-heartedly into political action in the Party most suited to their desires. A third way, the compromise road now being followed, has aroused the enmity of the two older Parties without gaining the full friendship of Labour.

CHAPTER SIX

REFERENCES

[1] The chief complaints of the Movement against Government discrimination were : (1) the plan of food control allocated supplies on the basis of pre-war trade, failing to take into account the increases in Co-operative membership due to their " non-profiteering " policy ; (2) an excess profits tax was levied on the Co-operative surplus which co-operators have always maintained was a sort of mutual saving ; (3) military tribunals determining the application of draft exemptions were allegedly loaded with private traders who disrupted Co-operative stores by sending key employees to the war ; (4) Co-operative societies were not given representation on the various emergency committees formed to control commodities of vital importance to the Movement.—Sidney and Beatrice Webb, *The Consumers' Co-operative Movement* (London, 1921), pp. 266-9.

[2] Alfred Barnes, *The Political Aspect of Co-operation* (Manchester, 1926), pp. 51-3.

[3] See Alfred Barnes, *The Proposed Labour and Co-operative Political Agreement* (Manchester, 1927), pp. 6-7.

[4] The president of the Co-operative Congress of 1935 declared : " We have the largest single political party in the country. We are prepared to march shoulder to shoulder with our friends in the Labour Party, but we are not prepared to lose our identity."—*Report of the Proceedings of the Sixty-seventh Annual Co-operative Congress, 1935*, p. 385.

[5] See *Report of the Annual Conference of the Co-operative Party, Nottingham, 1933*, p. 6 ; G. H. Workman, " Guild Affiliation to the Co-operative Party ", *The Co-operative Guildsman*, Vol. v (August 1932), p. 74.

[6] See *1936 Conference*, pp. 87-9 ; also *Report Proceedings of Sixty-ninth Annual Co-operative Congress, Bath, 1937*, pp. 450-1, 490-1.

[7] Evidence that Co-operative politicians are dissatisfied with the present subordinate status of the Co-operative Party is contained in the resolution submitted by the London Society to the 1936 Co-operative Congress. It provided that : (1) the Party have power to appoint and determine the duties of its own staff ; (2) the Party have authority to submit resolutions directly to the Co-operative Congress ; and (3) the contribution of the Co-operative Union to the Party be fixed at a five year average. *The Report of the Central Board to the Sixty-eighth Annual Congress of the Co-operative Union, Newcastle-upon-Tyne, 1936*, p. 200. The resolution was withdrawn and a compromise resolution offered by the Central Board was adopted. It provided for a special committee to study the Party and make recommendations to the 1937 Congress. This committee was not prepared to report at the time of the 1937 Congress.

[8] *Co-operative Party Constitution* (Manchester, 1928), pp. 2-3. During 1934, the National Committee met six times and the Executive Committee met twelve times. *Report of the National Committee of the Co-operative Party to the Annual Conference, 1935, at Southport*, p. 2.

[9] See *Model Constitution for Local Co-operative Parties* (London, n.d.) ; and *A Few Hints on the Formation of a Local Co-operative Party* (London, n.d.).

[10] The number of local Parties in 1935 was reported as 154, not including Constituency Parties existing within the area of a central Party. *Report of the National Committee of the Co-operative Party to the Annual Conference, 1936, at Great Yarmouth*, p. 10. The Party Secretary was unable to answer a questioner at the 1936 Conference who enquired the number of individual members in the

local Parties. *Report of the Co-operative Party Annual Conference Proceedings, 1936,* p. 13.

[11] *Co-operative Party Report to the Annual Conference, Great Yarmouth, 1936,* p. 3.

[12] *The Report of the Central Board to the Sixty-eighth Annual Congress of the Co-operative Union, Newcastle-upon-Tyne, 1936,* p. 385 ; the exact expenditure reported was £5,989 13s.

[13] *Report of the Co-operative Party Annual Conference Proceedings, 1936,* p. 19.

[14] *Ibid.,* p. 12.

[15] *Annual Report of the Co-operative Party, to the National Conference, 1935,* p. 2.

[16] *Twenty-ninth Report and Balance Sheet of the London Co-operative Society, Ltd., for the Year Ended September 7th, 1935,* p. 14.

[17] *Report of the Political Committee to the Ninth Annual Conference of the London Co-operative Party, 1935,* p. 4.

[18] *The Work of the London Labour Party, 1932-3,* p. 16.

[19] *Report of the Political Committee to the Ninth Annual Conference of the London Co-operative Party, 1935,* pp. 1-3.

[20] *Political Purposes Committee Report on the Administration of the Political Fund, 1935,* issued by the Royal Arsenal Co-operative Society, p. 5.

[21] *Ibid.,* pp. 7-10.

[22] *Ibid.,* p. 12.

[23] T. W. Mercer, *Co-operative Representatives in Parliament* (Manchester, 1924), p. 5.

[24] *Report Proceedings of Sixty-ninth Annual Co-operative Congress, Bath, 1937,* p. 491.

PART III
THE PARTY IN ACTION

LEADERSHIP OF THE LABOUR PARTY, 1931-7

A. THE OLIGARCHY OF THE " BIG FIVE "

THE story of Labour Party leadership from 1922 to 1931 provides an example of what a continental student of political parties has designated the " oligarchical tendency ".[1] The Ramsay MacDonald legend was built up steadily following his return to the House of Commons in 1922. He won the Leadership of the Party by making gestures which met the approval of the " left ", especially the " Wild Men of the Clyde ", who came from Scotland determined to sweep traditions and gentility aside. As Laski has written, MacDonald's pacifist record made him seem, to the Clydesiders in 1922, a " symbol of their own extremism ".[2] His position as the Leader of His Majesty's Opposition and his oratorical skill made him the champion of the war-tired working class ; his grace and charm attracted middle-class Liberals to the Labour standard. The veneration of the crowd continued after the fall of the first Labour Government, but his colleagues were impatient over his alleged compromises and blunders. For the five years of Tory rule after 1924, one of his biographers records, a common topic of conversation at informal gatherings of Labour People concerned the former Prime Minister and the task of finding a Leader to succeed him .[3]

But MacDonald was no dictator. During his periods as Premier he exercised the usual prerogatives of that office. Throughout the decade before 1931 there were other strong leaders with considerable followings in sections of the Party. Philip Snowden's abilities were widely acclaimed and his caustic debating skill made him very popular on the public platform. Arthur Henderson held the strategic post of Party Secretary, and his long period of solid leadership had won the gratitude of both Trade Unionists and local Party workers. J. H. Thomas, supported by the railwaymen, quickly acquired the social finesse of court and well-to-do circles, a virtue which was admired by many of his former Cabinet colleagues. The last of the " Big Five " was J. R. Clynes, whose Leadership of the Party in the House from 1918 to 1922 was creditable, and whose powerful Municipal and General Workers' Union was the second in size in the Party.

It was this group of five which planned the formation of the second Labour Government and, to a large extent, chose its personnel. In the group there was some jealousy and temperament ; the account of their wrangling in Viscount Snowden's recent autobiography exposed an almost childish rivalry among them.

During the " General Strike " of 1926 and after, the leaders demonstrated a capacity to drift along with the rank and file of the Labour Movement. The agitations of James Maxton and A. J. Cook for a

Socialist revival in 1927-8 projected into sharp relief the essential " right " tendencies of the official leadership of the Party.   MacDonald and Snowden left the Independent Labour Party, which they had done so much to build ; the other three chief Party leaders were regarded as " safe and sane " Trade Unionists.   The second Labour Government was overwhelmingly made up of conservative elements of the Party.   Of the " left " faction, only George Lansbury and Sir Oswald Mosley were admitted to Government posts of responsibility, and both of them were confined to minor offices.   Events soon caused Mosley to resign from the Government and begin the " New Party", which was the forerunner of the British Union of Fascists. Lansbury was sorely troubled with the trend of events, but remained in the Cabinet.

The split of the Party in 1931 was not a clear-cut one between " right " and " left ", but rather more complicated.   MacDonald and Thomas found themselves more nearly in harmony with their Conservative opponents than with their Labour Party colleagues.   Snowden joined the new Government because he doubtless was convinced that economies were necessary and that his job was to remain until they were made.   Perhaps the great hostility of Trade Union interests towards the proposed cuts in unemployment benefits and social services were among the deciding influences which served to keep Henderson and Clynes out of the Coalition.   Such " left " elements as there were in the Party remained for the time being.

B. Elder Leaders Remaining after 1931

During the campaign of 1931 a determined effort had been made to build up Arthur Henderson, to dramatize his solidity, and to glorify his very considerable achievements as Foreign Secretary. As Opposition Leader since the formation of the National Government, he was the prospective Prime Minister ; as the important Party figure who remained faithful to Labour, he became a rallying point for many bewildered workers. In spite of his failure to secure election to the House, Henderson was chosen as Leader, and Lansbury became Chairman of the Parliamentary Labour Party.

Henderson was occupied after February 1932, at Geneva with his work as President of the World Disarmament Conference. During a recess in the Conference, he fought and won a by-election, but both ill-health and his work at Geneva prevented his accepting the active Leadership in the House again. Already near seventy years of age, " Uncle Arthur " never resumed a dominant role in Party affairs, although the prestige of his name continued to be a great asset to the Party. In October 1932, Henderson asked to be relieved of the title of Leader. Ill-health compelled him to resign as Secretary to the Party in May 1934. His death in October 1935 ended a distinguished career of devoted work for his twin great causes, socialism and peace.[4]

The task of leading Labour's scant forces in the House of Commons from 1931 to 1935 fell on the shoulders of George Lansbury, one of the oldest and

most picturesque figures in the Party. This " grand
old man " probably was already the most beloved
figure in the British Labour Movement. He is
sentimental and enthusiastic, a fervent Socialist who
might have remained untested by major responsibility
except for the events of 1931 which swept him to
unexpected Leadership after he had entered his
seventh decade. As Leader, he was eloquent in
debate, an alert champion of the rights of every Labour
Member, and a tireless exponent of his Party's faith
up and down the country.[5]   Although himself a
convinced " left-winger ", Lansbury subordinated his
personal convictions on many matters in order that he
might express the Party's official opinion.   Only when
he was faced with compromising his own strong
pacifist views in 1935, did he balk and relinquish the
Leadership to C. R. Attlee, the Vice-Chairman of the
Parliamentary Party.   Lansbury made few contributions to Party policy.   His chief work was the
marshalling of Labour's small group in the House of
Commons into an effective Opposition.

Mr J. R. Clynes, who was defeated in 1931, but
managed to regain his seat in 1935, is a moderate centre
Labour leader who served in the war-time Coalition
Government and in both Labour Cabinets.[6]   He is
steady and dependable, but lacks the personality and
the youth to undertake the Party Leadership.   He
occupied the front bench after 1935, but his participation in debate is undistinguished.   His importance to
the Party is based more on his close association with the
powerful National Union of General and Municipal

Workers, and his ability to interpret the Trade Union point of view in the National Executive.

C. New Trends in Party Leadership

A change of very great significance has taken place in the nature of Labour Party Leadership since 1931. About one-half of the 1929-31 Cabinet was composed of persons of working class origin, who had been denied the opportunity of higher education. All of the " Big Five " were born into poor families ; all climbed to leadership in the Party through years of Trade Union and Socialist work.

If the Labour Party should be called upon to form a Government after the next General Election, its chief Ministers would be drawn from a wholly different background, for the leading active Trade Unionists are confining themselves to their industrial work and remaining outside of Parliament. Except for Mr Herbert Morrison, former Minister of Transport, and Emanuel Shinwell, ex-Minister of Mines and victor over Ramsay MacDonald at Seaham in 1935, most of the outstanding Labourites in Parliament are of either bourgeois or aristocratic origin.

Nearly all have received University education ; several hold advanced degrees. Their occupations differ widely from those of leaders in the pre-1931 era. Both C. R. Attlee, present Leader, and Dr Hugh Dalton, Under Secretary for Foreign Affairs under Henderson, are barristers and both are former teachers at the London School of Economics ; Arthur Greenwood, who was Minister of Health, came to Party work from a lectureship in economics ; H. B. Lees-Smith, ex-President of the Board of Education, teaches politics at the London School of Economics ; Sir Stafford Cripps and D. N. Pritt are counted among the most distinguished lawyers in Britain ; A. V. Alexander, former First Lord of the Admiralty, entered Co-operative political work from the secondary education field ; Tom Johnston, ex-Lord Privy Seal, is a journalist and author ; Lord Addison is a distinguished authority on anatomy and physiology ; Philip Noel-Baker has served as University lecturer and publicist.

For the Labour Party, this rather surprising change has both advantages and disadvantages. The technical and academic training of the new leaders is of value in the day to day work of the Opposition, and will be a great asset if Labour forms another Government. The danger that Leaders will be won over by the enemy through social favours and the " aristocratic embrace " is minimized. The new leadership has increased the prestige of the Party, particularly among the middle class voters.

On the other hand, there are drawbacks to the situation. It is often alleged that men from comfortable homes can never have as vivid a picture of the sufferings and privations of the working class as those who have lived in poverty themselves. More important, however, is the danger that the powerful Trade Union leaders who remain outside of Parliament will attempt to dictate policy to a Labour Government. Such action would subject the Party to much justifiable criticism.

D. Present Contenders for Leadership

One of the most serious weaknesses in Labour's present strategic position is its failure to advance a Leader who can measure up to the electorate's standard for a Prime Minister. MacDonald is gone, and no one has been able to fill his place. Of a half-dozen potential leaders, none has emerged as a dominant national figure with the confidence of the Movement behind him. The chief contenders for Leadership of the Party are : Major Clement R. Attlee, Herbert Morrison, Arthur Greenwood, Dr Hugh Dalton and Sir Stafford Cripps.

Major Attlee, present Leader of the Party, was trained as a barrister, but turned first to social work in East London, and then to Socialist political activity. His rise in politics was rapid, due to a remarkably favourable series of circumstances. Directly after returning from the war, he was elected Alderman and Mayor in Stepney, an East London Borough. He entered Parliament in 1922, and at once became Parliamentary Private Secretary to Mr. MacDonald; in the 1924 Labour Government he was Under Secretary for War.

On Sir Oswald Mosley's resignation from the second Labour Government in 1930, Attlee was appointed to his post as Chancellor of the Duchy of Lancaster. When Sir Charles Trevelyan left the Cabinet early in 1931, Mr H. B. Lees-Smith was appointed President of the Board of Education, and Attlee succeeded him as Postmaster-General. In the Election of 1931,

Attlee managed to hold his seat by a 500-vote margin. In the new Parliament, only Lansbury ranked ahead of him on the Labour benches, and he was elected Deputy Leader. Lansbury had an accident in December 1933, which gave Attlee several months as Acting Leader, and Lansbury's resignation on the eve of the 1935 Election placed the Leadership in Attlee's hands.

Attlee carried the unexpected burden creditably through the campaign, but he then was regarded widely as just filling in. In the new Parliament none of the three contenders for the Leadership—Attlee, Morrison, or Greenwood—obtained a majority on the first ballot. Attlee led with fifty-eight votes, Morrison second with forty-four, and Greenwood thirty-three. On a second vote, confined to the two leading candidates, Attlee received eighty-eight votes and Morrison forty-eight. Morrison then withdrew, Greenwood accepted the Deputy Leadership, and Attlee continued as Leader.

Although respected by his colleagues in the Parliamentary Party, Attlee has not yet been dramatized sufficiently to become a great national figure. As the *New Statesman and Nation* says : " He is a natural Adjutant, but not a General." In personal relations he is almost shy ; on the platform he is sincere, at times forceful. His socialism is left of centre, and before he assumed the Leadership he did not hesitate to pronounce opinions which were unpopular with Transport House officialdom. Attlee has done well in a most difficult situation ; he is not the " strong man " demanded by many, but he has a reserved, intellectual approach which may be more fitting for the Labour Party at this time.   His recent book, *The Labour Party in Perspective*, contains an admirably frank discussion of Labour's problems.

Herbert Morrison, former Minister of Transport, Leader of the London County Council, and Secretary of the London Labour Party, is a unique figure in the Labour Movement.   He was born in East London, and received only an elementary school education. Morrison started work as an errand boy, and moved from one job to another, bettering his economic status. The death of the Secretary of the London Labour Party during its first year of existence, led to the appointment of the twenty-seven year old Morrison in 1915.   In the twenty-two years since he assumed the task of building a Central Party in London, Morrison has grown tremendously.   Years of experience as Leader of Opposition at County Hall gave him an intimate knowledge of London's municipal problems. During 1920-1 he served as Mayor of Hackney, his London Borough.

His parliamentary experience, however, is limited ; he won South Hackney in 1923, but lost it in 1924 ; recaptured it in 1929, was defeated in 1931, but won in 1935.   In the second Labour Government he was an outstanding success as Minister of Transport.   An unnamed writer has declared : " . . . no Cabinet Minister has inspired a Department with so much zest and efficiency since Winston Churchill was at the Home Office before the war."[7]   Appointed to the post because of his long experience in London's traffic controversies, he was responsible for legislation to take over the metropolitan transport facilities, and skilfully brought the bill to an advanced stage before the fall of the Government. It was subsequently enacted in amended form by the National Government. Before the fall of the Labour Government, he was included in the Cabinet. In 1934, when Labour obtained a majority on the London County Council, Morrison as its Leader became London's first Socialist " Prime Minister ". The skill with which he put his colleagues to work is eloquent testimony of his ability as a leader. Much of the credit for Labour's second L.C.C. victory (1937) belongs to this aggressive Leader.

Morrison is a moderate Socialist (his critics say a Liberal), a practical man who glorifies administrative efficiency, yet possesses rare political acumen. He has a powerful will and an aggressive nature, but this is blended with a certain shrewdness which causes him to compromise when necessary to achieve his end. He believes that the best course for the labour Party is to win the confidence of the people by administering public business efficiently and showing that socialization can be accomplished without upsetting the apple cart. For example, he chose to proceed with the London transport scheme in spite of the fact that the price of its passage was the assurance of a rather high rate of interest to the stockholders of the operating companies.

He is an exponent of the public corporation form for socialized industries, with an expert board chosen for ability alone. Believing that there are definite financial limitations upon the extension of the social services under the present system, Morrison holds that the next

Labour Government should devote itself chiefly to the socialization of half a dozen major industries.

His present position in the Party is strong. The failure of the Parliamentary Party to select him as Leader in the new Parliament of 1935 may have been due to these three factors : (1) the feeling that he should continue his work in the London County Council ; (2) the fact that he antagonized powerful Trade Union leaders by his firm opposition to the principle of workers' representation on the governing boards of socialized industries; and (3) the "left-wing's" distrust of his reassurances to the capitalists that Labour really means no harm, his willingness to compromise on essential matters of compensation and valuation, and his refusal to state bluntly the full implications of a Socialist majority in the House of Commons. But Morrison does possess tested qualities of leadership and a personality which might be dramatized to the electorate as a " strong man ", in spite of a certain deficiency in personal warmth and magnetism.

Arthur Greenwood, head of the Labour Party Research Department and former Minister of Health, is now Deputy Leader of the House. He entered Parliament in 1922 after several years of teaching economics in the University of Leeds. He carries an important share of Party work in Parliament ; he has rendered valuable service in research. Although personally likeable and well equipped, Greenwood appears as an unlikely choice for the command of Labour's forces.

The fourth major leader of the Parliamentary Party is Dr Hugh Dalton, who was Under Secretary for

Foreign Affairs in the second Labour Government. He did not enter Parliament until 1924, but assumed a place of prominence at once partially by virtue of his academic work in the field of public finance. His prestige was enhanced further by his association with Arthur Henderson in the Foreign Office. After his defeat in 1931, he maintained contact with the Party through his membership on the Executive, and took a leading part in framing of Party policy. His book, *Practical Socialism for Britain*, was regarded as an authoritative statement of general Labour policy. Dr Dalton's particular contribution to the Party lies in his ability to express the views of the majority neatly and eloquently. At the Party Conference, on the Executive, and in the House of Commons, Dalton is gaining ground. His connection with the London School of Economics has augmented considerably his prestige. His term as Chairman of the Executive (1936-7) focused added attention on his work and record. He appears destined for high Cabinet office if another Labour Government is formed, and may some day become a compromise Leader.

Sir Stafford Cripps has been active in the Labour Party only eight years, yet he has been an important national figure during the whole of that period. The second Labour Government seriously needed a barrister of ability to take the post of Solicitor-General, and in 1930 selected Cripps, a lawyer with a large practice, and the son of Lord Parmoor, the Lord President of the Council. He won a by-election in January 1931, and at once took over an important share of Government work in the House. One of the few Government men to survive in the Election of 1931, Sir Stafford's ability was most outstanding in the 1931-5 Parliament.

Although new to the Movement, Sir Stafford moved swiftly to the "left". When the Independent Labour Party seceded, he aided E. F. Wise, William Mellor, and others in organizing the "affiliationists" into the Socialist League, a propagandist group within the Labour Party. Cripps' ideas were spread through the activities of this group, until its expulsion from the Party and dissolution in 1937. He advocates telling the electorate what the Party intends to do, and he wants the next Labour Government to proceed rapidly to socialism. Under his plan, the chief agencies of economic power would be taken over at once by the new Government, unconstitutional opposition would be met with force, and the transition to socialism achieved by semi-parliamentary means.

Cripps has great personal gifts ; he has a sparkling intellect and is a direct, forceful, though unemotional speaker ; few barristers in Britain approach him in legal learning ; he is widely respected for his honesty and selflessness. Sir Stafford was born into a wealthy family, and has a large personal fortune which he spends freely for the "cause". He is handicapped by his tendency to minor indiscretions on the platform, which provide the Tories with numerous extreme statements for campaign leaflets on Socialist designs. His radicalism has prevented his assumption of Leadership in the Party. He moved to the back-benches with George Lansbury in 1935 because of his disagreement with the Party's official stand on sanctions and since then has been out of official Party favour most of the time.   The Party's expulsion of the Socialist League and its subsequent dissolution severely tested his Labour loyalty.   Elected to the Executive at the 1937 Conference, Cripps may now enter a new phase of service to the Labour Party.   If the trend of events drives Labour leftward, Sir Stafford Cripps may rise to Leadership of the Party.

E.   TRADE UNION LEADERS

The two Trade Unionists who loom most important in contemporary Party matters, Sir Walter Citrine and Ernest Bevin, are not Members of Parliament.

Sir Walter Citrine is Secretary of the Trades Union Congress and President of the International Federation of Trade Unions.   He rose to prominence in the Trade Union Movement through the Electrical Union.[8]   In 1918 he stood unsuccessfully for a parliamentary seat. After two years as Assistant and Acting Secretary, he was appointed Secretary of the Trades Union Congress in 1926.   Citrine's critics allege that he is conservative and a damper on militancy in the Trade Unions.   In fairness it should be pointed out that he bears a heavy responsibility both to his large Trade Unionist constituency and to the community.

Although the Trades Union Congress' voice in Party affairs has been expanded by increasing the Trade Union representation on the National Council of Labour, Citrine maintains that the Trades Union Congress has not given up its right to hold opinions on political questions. By virtue of his position, Sir Walter's influence over Party affairs is very great, and if Labour forms another Government, it probably will be exerted to direct the Party along lines of moderation rather than drastic socialization.

Mr Ernest Bevin, Secretary of the Transport and General Workers' Union, was described recently as " much the biggest man the Trade Union Movement has to-day—the only man who looks at all like a leader."[9] His Union is now second in size only to the mineworkers ; through his rough sort of ability he rose to its leadership from the Bristol docks. Bevin became a Socialist in his youth[10] ; at first he was a "left-winger ", but is now often classed with Citrine. He opposed vehemently the proposals of Cripps and the Socialist League, and recently fought for delaying the inauguration of the new method of selecting local Parties' representation on the National Executive.

Bevin stood unsuccessfully for Parliament in 1918 and 1931. In early 1931, he was frequently mentioned as a leading contender for the next Labour Prime Ministership. A prominent Labourite, after reviewing possible Leaders of the Party, wrote: "Of all these the most depends on the decision of Ernest Bevin, and the line he takes as regards politics."[11] Bevin was responsible to a considerable extent both for the forming on its present basis of his Union and for the reorganization of the *Daily Herald*. His service on the Macmillan Committee on Finance and Industry demonstrated that his ability exceeds the limits of his

Trade Union work. His entry into Parliament would mean the addition of an aggressive and vital force. In spite of his apparent decision to support the "right-wing" of the Party, Bevin is still a great unknown factor in Labour politics.

F. INTELLECTUALS AND THE LABOUR PARTY

Intellectuals have a unique place in British Labour politics. They are welcomed to Party membership, called upon as advisers in important matters, and are often given high places in Party and Parliament. It is a remarkable fact that the Labour Party has drawn into its fold some of the most distinguished intellectuals of Britain, far more than have either the Conservative or Liberals. J. A. Spender wrote in 1925 : " Conservatives positively dislike ' high brows ' and Liberals are not very easy with them, but Labour adores them. . . ."[12]

Sidney Webb's philosophy of gradualism still dominates the Party's political thought, although its founder has chosen to devote recent years to sympathetic investigation of its antithesis in the Soviet Union. Harold J. Laski, R. H. Tawney, C. M. Lloyd, and G. D. H. Cole have been active for many years. All four have made extremely important contributions to the Party. Laski is a frequent Labour platform figure, and devotes much of his time to writing and speaking for the Labour cause. Tawney's role is less prominent, but he constantly renders services for the Party in framing policy and advising on educational matters. Cole is one of the Party's leading theorists and most outspoken critics.

There is a younger generation of intellectuals in the Labour Party which plays a much different role from that of Cole, Laski, Lloyd, and Tawney. It is composed chiefly of men in their thirties ; some of them teach at Oxford, Cambridge, or London ; they are moderates who contribute, not only theories, but largely technical data in their specialized fields. Unlike the older intellectuals, most of this group stand for Parliament regularly ; they have been given difficult seats to fight, but most of them will probably secure admission to the House before long. Some of the best research and hardest work on problems of a future Labour Government have come from this group, which includes : Colin Clark, R. H. S. Crossman, Robert Fraser, Douglas Jay, E. F. M. Durbin, Hugh Gaitskell, John Parker, Ivor Thomas, and others. Their efforts have been co-ordinated through the New Fabian Research Bureau, and their individual contributions may be found in *New Trends in Socialism*, edited by G. E. G. Catlin.

G. The " Aristocratic Embrace "

The temptations of respectability and power which seek to divert Socialist leaders from their tasks aptly has been termed by the *New Statesman and Nation* the " aristocratic embrace ". Social pressure was a factor in three group defections which the Party has experienced. Several Labour spokesmen, important and minor, deserted to the Liberals during the Party's early years. George Barnes, John Hodge, and others never returned after participation in the wartime

Coalition Government. Ramsay MacDonald, J. H. Thomas, and Philip Snowden joined the ranks of the Party's opponents in 1931. Even more significant, however, are the numerous cases in which Labour leaders have been disarmed and rendered useless to the Party, though remaining in it.

The susceptibility of Labourites to the charms of the " embrace " is due partially to the persistence of and the respect for the aristocratic class in Britain. Some workers still speak of their " betters " and respect their " superiors " ; many accept the system of snobbery, and envy and imitate the upper classes. When a Labourite of lowly birth enters the House of Commons, the lure of upper class respectability is flaunted before him and is available to him. If he becomes a figure of importance, he may mingle with the " great and famous at Court, the club, the drawing-room, and the country house ".[13] If there is a grain of vanity in those who achieve high positions, it is likely to be exploited.

Nowhere, perhaps, does the " embrace " operate with such effect as in the House of Commons. One Conservative Member has described the " atmosphere " in these words :[14]

In the British Parliament, political differences do not prevent personal friendships, and in the smoking room and libraries bitter antagonists on the floor of the House discuss their disagreement with complete candour and understanding. The House has a corporate sense transcending party which no West End club possesses. . . . What separates us as party men is less than what unites us as countrymen.

One critic of the Labour Party has maintained that the " decline " of the Party began in 1906, when the new Labour Members of Parliament first began to ape bourgeois statesmen.[15] Another is convinced that the real " betrayal " occurred in early 1923, when the Labour group accepted the social and political conventions of the House.[16] Decisions were made at both times which unquestionably opened the way to influences which diluted the zeal of the leaders for radical changes. The autobiographies of some of the older Labour leaders unconsciously reveal the transformation in the attitudes of one time revolutionaries.

The recently published autobiography of David Kirkwood, one of the most colourful " Wild Men of the Clyde ", reveals how subtle and effective is the " atmosphere " of the House of Commons in soothing radicals. When the Labour Party swept Glasgow in 1922, the ten resolute Socialists elected to Parliament made a solemn declaration which included a pledge that, " In all things they will abjure vanity and self-aggrandizement. . . ."[17] Kirkwood was determined to smash tradition and formalities. After the Clyde group made attacks on the Prime Minister (Mr Bonar Law), Law told Kirkwood it was " fine to hear your Glasgow accent ".[18] Kirkwood called Mr Stanley Baldwin " a Uriah Heep " in debate, and afterwards Mr Baldwin asked him, " Have I appeared like that to you ? "[19] Later, Kirkwood announced he would make a violent attack on Mr Lloyd George, and received a letter from him apologizing because he could not be at the House to hear it.[20]

Since the MacDonald-Thomas defection, the Movement has experienced only one major controversy over the " embrace ". In the King's Jubilee honours list of June 1935, Charles Edwards, Chief Whip of the Labour Party, Walter Citrine, Secretary of the Trades Union Congress, and Arthur Pugh, Secretary of the Iron and Steel Association, were knighted. There was a storm of disapproval throughout the Labour Movement. Declaring that the whole business of political honours " stinks with snobbery ", Professor Tawney asked what the public would believe of the Party's professions of social equality " if prominent members of the Party sit up, like poodles in a drawing-room, wag their tails when patted, and lick their lips at the social sugar-plums tossed them by their masters " ?[21] Acceptances of knighthoods from a Conservative Government demonstrate the profound respect which some Britishers have for social position ; the Trades Union Congress refused to censure the Trade Unionists, but the Labour Party Conference ordered the Executive to investigate and report, then rejected in 1936 the Executive's " whitewashing " report.

The problem is one which is declining in importance, because the leadership of the Party is clearly shifting to persons of non-working class origin. As an old Tory is alleged to have written to a young Tory, " It is always your middle class revolutionary who is difficult to handle. He is used to good manners and is not affected by them."[22] Even so, social pressure remains as one of the most powerful weapons in the hands of the Labour Party's opponents.

CHAPTER SEVEN

REFERENCES

[1] Robert Michels, *Political Parties : A Sociological Study of the Oligarchical Tendencies of Modern Democracy* (London, 1915), pp. 54 ff.

[2] Harold J. Laski, " Ramsay MacDonald : A Portrait ", *Harpers*, Vol. clxiv (May 1932), p. 754.

[3] Mary A. Hamilton, *J. Ramsay MacDonald* (London, 1929), pp. 290 ff.

[4] See E. A. Jenkins, *From Foundry to Foreign Office* (London, 1933) ; C. M. Lloyd, " Uncle Arthur ", in *New Statesman and Nation*, Vol. x (October 26th, 1935), pp. 591-2.

[5] Dr Christopher Addison, " Labour's Grand Old Man ", *New Clarion*, Vol. ii (January 7th, 1933), p. 83. For the life and work of Mr Lansbury, see George Lansbury, *My Life* (London, 1928) ; George Lansbury, *My England* (London, 1934) ; Edgar Lansbury, *George Lansbury, My Father* (London, 1934).

[6] See J. R. Clynes, *Memoirs*, Vol. i, 1869-1924 (London, 1937).

[7] *New Statesman and Nation*, Vol. x (November 23rd, 1935), p. 764.

[8] Biographical data drawn in part from R. B. Suthers, " The Trades Union Congress ", *Labour Magazine*, Vol. xi (September 1932), pp. 205-6.

[9] *New Statesman and Nation*, Vol. viii (December 30th, 1933), p. 870.

[10] Biographical data drawn in part from R. B. Suthers, " The Transport and General Workers Union ", *Labour Magazine*, Vol. x (September 1931), p. 204 ; also from *Labour*, Vol. iv (October 1936), p. 38.

[11] A. L. Rowse, *Politics and the Younger Generation* (London, 1931), p. 97.

[12] J. A. Spender, *The Public Life*, Vol. i (London, 1925), p. 159.

[13] John M. Gaus, *Great Britain : A Study of Civic Loyalty* (Chicago, 1929), p. 126.

[14] Hugh Molson, M.P., " The Future of the Constitution " in *Conservatism and the Future* (London, 1935), p. 245.

[15] Shaw Desmond, *Labour : The Giant with Feet of Clay* (Glasgow, 1921), p. 86.

[16] John Scanlon, *Decline and Fall of the Labour Party* (London, 1932), p. 39.

[17] David Kirkwood, *My Life of Revolt* (London, 1935), pp. 192-3.

[18] *Ibid.*, p. 202.

[19] *Ibid.*, p. 204.

[20] *Ibid.*, p. 206.

[21] *New Statesman and Nation*, Vol. ix (June 22nd, 1935), p. 922.

[22] *New Statesman and Nation*, Vol. x (December 16th, 1935), p. 724. Both De Man and Michels have pointed out that bourgeois socialists are less susceptible to temptations and environment. Robert Michels, *op. cit.*, pp. 307-8 ; Henry De Man, *Psychology of Socialism* (London, 1928), p. 235.

THE PARLIAMENTARY LABOUR PARTY

A. THE POSITION OF THE PARLIAMENTARY LABOUR GROUP

THE Labour Members of Parliament form a relatively independent and nearly autonomous group called the Parliamentary Labour Party. It chooses the Leader of the Party, determines the Party attitude toward specific pieces of legislation, and, to a great extent, is the Labour Party in the eyes of the country. Between the dissolution for an Election and the assembling of Parliament afterwards, the Party machine is all important. The Executive, the Central Office, and the local Parties devote themselves to organizing and financing the campaign ; all efforts are directed toward obtaining as many seats in the House of Commons as possible. After the Election, however, the Party organization becomes, to a large extent, the servant of the results of its efforts, the Labour group in Parliament.

The controls of the Labour Party over the Parliamentary Party are few. If the Labour group in the House of Commons flagrantly disregarded the policy declarations of the Annual Conference, there might conceivably come a time when the Conference or Executive would take drastic action, such as wholesale expulsion of individuals from the Party, or refusal to endorse the candidacies of offending M.P.s. Such a crisis has not arisen. The interlocking membership of the Executive and the Parliamentary Party renders unlikely a serious conflict over policy between the two bodies. The Labour Party's constitutional provision that official parliamentary candidates must accept and conform to the " Constitution, Programme, Principles and Policy of the Party " constitutes a general restriction on the Parliamentary Party's freedom of action. Provision is made in the Party Constitution for the issue of a manifesto before each Election ; the Executive and the Parliamentary Party Executive Committee jointly decide which items of the Party's programme shall be included in it.

The federal structure of the Labour Party exposes the independence of the Parliamentary Party to intermittent threats by organizations affiliated nationally. Between the Election of 1929 and the formation of the second Labour Government, the request of the Trades Union Congress leaders for a consultation was rejected by the leaders of the Parliamentary Party,[1] though Trade Unionists were deeply involved in the fall of the Government in 1931. There is a significant tendency, however, for the Trade Unions to increase their external control over the Parliamentary Party. This influence is exerted chiefly through their majority on the National Council of Labour.

When the Italo-Abyssinian crisis arose, a meeting of the Party Executive and General Council of the Trades Union Congress was called at Margate on the eve of the Congress session there. George Lansbury, as Leader of the Party, protested that the Labour group in the House should be represented, and the meeting was expanded to include Parliamentary Party representatives. Lansbury's subsequent resignation was due not primarily to a disagreement between himself and the Parliamentary Party, but rather because of his differences with the leaders of other sections of the Labour Movement.

Although Mr Bassett may have overstated the danger when he declared recently that any " measure of control, formal or informal, exercised over parliamentary parties by extra-parliamentary bodies vitiates the democratic process ",[2] nevertheless it is undesirable that Members of Parliament should be subject to extensive non-Party controls. The Labour Party's scheme of allowing affiliated organizations to finance its candidates (within certain limits) facilitates the possibility of outside influence on legislators. Under such circumstances the Member of Parliament has not only his obligations to the Party and to his constituents, but also a third loyalty to the organization which sponsored his candidacy. The latter obligation is often paramount because many Trade Unionists, for example, are dependent for their economic and political future upon continued harmonious relationships with their Unions. The sponsoring organization may take an extremely narrow or selfish view on a particular issue and bring effective pressure on " its " M.P. to the exclusion of the broader interests of constituency, Party, and conscience.

B. Organization of the Labour Party in Parliament

The Parliamentary Labour Party in 1936 celebrated its thirtieth birthday. Although there were Labour Members in the House of Commons before, it was not until 1906 with the election of twenty-nine Labour Members of Parliament that the group was organized on a regular Party basis. Keir Hardie was elected Chairman ; Whips were appointed ; and an office was set up in the House of Commons.3 The work of the Parliamentary Party was conducted on an exceedingly democratic basis. There was a weekly full Party meeting for the discussion of parliamentary work, the consideration of Party committee reports, and the selection of official speakers on the Bills before the House. In the pre-war period, all Labour speakers were deemed official and had to be authorized by the Parliamentary Party, but in recent years only front bench speakers are arranged officially by the Party.

Standing committees were appointed to deal systematically with Party business. At the opening of each session, the Party group reviewed past Conference resolutions, and made them the basis of the Party's legislative programme. The National Party Executive met jointly with the Parliamentary Party to compile a list of Party Bills and motions, and the individual Members of Parliament were required to put forward the agreed Party business if they were successful in the "ballot" for Bills—the method used to determine order of priority for introduction of Private Members' Bills.

The procedure within the Parliamentary Party changed little until the formation of the first Labour Government following the Election of 1923. Then the customary Cabinet control was substituted for the authority of the Party meeting ; an elected group of twelve Members not in the Government was joined by three Ministers to form a sort of liaison committee.[4] In the short period Labour was in power, no serious disagreement between the Cabinet and the Parliamentary Party was made public.

During the succeeding years of Conservative Government, the Parliamentary Party reverted to the usual organization, with an Executive Committee composed of the Chairman, Deputy Chairman, Chief Whip, and twelve other committee-men, which met daily to discuss the business coming before the House. Full Party meetings retained the power to make final decisions. The handful of Labour Lords were invited to the Party meetings, and one of their number was placed on the Executive Committee.[5]

Under the second Labour Government the democratic process was pushed again into the background. The Cabinet assumed control and, as in 1924, a consultative committee composed of non-Government Members met with three Ministers, establishing an official agency for contact between the Government and the Labour back benchers. The weekly Party meetings apparently were handled so badly that Members were driven into revolt against the Government. Justifying their action on the necessity for secrecy, Ministers introduced legislation and expected support without consulting the Party meeting ; when Labour Members disagreed with Cabinet policy, they were termed disloyal and disciplinary action was discussed.[6] This strained relationship was an important factor in the crisis of 1931, for the confidence of a large group of Labour Members had been shaken by the internal disagreements.

As the Opposition again, Labour reorganized on democratic lines. The group of forty-six Members remaining in the Commons after the 1931 Election and the I.L.P. disaffiliation held regular meetings on Tuesday afternoons. There were daily meetings of the Executive Committee, which was composed of the Chairman, Vice-Chairman, Chief Whip, a representative of the Labour Lords, and seven others. It made recommendations on procedure, and the full Party meeting, after discussion, voted on the course to follow. The same organization is used by the present Parliamentary Party, except the Executive Committee has been expanded by five additional Members, now including the officers, the Lords' representative, and twelve others.

Under the Standing Orders of the Parliamentary Party, the majority view is the Party view, and all Members are bound to vote with it unless they have conscientious scruples, in which case they may refrain from voting. Members are allowed a free hand on Private Members' Bills and motions which do not affect Party policy. If Members have doubts on Party policy, they are expected to raise them at Party meetings.   Divisions must not be called without informing the Whips and obtaining the approval of the leaders in charge.   In rare cases affecting Party policy Members may be given a free hand, provided that they make it clear their opinion is personal, and that they refrain from attacks on other Members of the Party, and do not challenge a division without official approval.   In addition, Members must submit to the Executive Committee or Party meeting all motions, Bills, and amendments that in any way affect Party policy or tactics.

The Parliamentary Party committees are adjusted each session according to the business of the House. The number of regular committees varies between five and ten.   Their Chairmen are usually members of the Executive Committee and the personnel of the Parliamentary Party committees generally includes the Labour Members on the corresponding House of Commons Committee.   The parliamentary group also relies for guidance and research on the policy committee of the National Executive and on its various sub-committees.

C.   Officers of the Parliamentary Party

It is the established practice of the Labour Party that the Chairman of the Parliamentary Party serves also as Leader.   Only for a year after the 1931 Election were the posts divided ; Arthur Henderson continued as Leader of His Majesty's Opposition despite his defeat, and George Lansbury was Chairman of the Parliamentary Labour Party.   After October 1932, however, the Party returned to the usual practice of combining the two posts. When Labour forms a Government, its Leader, of course, becomes Prime Minister. When Labour is the chief Party of the Opposition, the Leader, under the terms of the recent legislation on Ministers' and Members' salaries, receives a salary from the State.

The Leader of the Labour Party is an influential figure, but has not the great powers which the Leader of the Conservative Party enjoys. Neither may he commit the Party to future action by his statements, nor is he given control of the Party machine. The Labour Party is committed officially only through its regular democratic procedure. Chance that the Party may be bound by the Leader in an emergency has been largely eliminated by the extension of the National Council of Labour's authority.

It is customary for the Leader to keep within the bounds of Party policy, as determined in Conferences and interpreted by the Parliamentary Party, the National Executive, and the National Council of Labour. The subordination of personal views by the Leader is deemed necessary, even in Party Conferences, to preserve the front of unity to the public. George Lansbury's statement to the 1935 Conference on sanctions clearly reveals the usual concept of the Leader as official spokesman :[7]

Often—and only the Executive and my colleagues know how often—I have disagreed with their policy, and because I was a member of the Executive, and lately because of my other position (Leader), I have remained silent during the whole of the Conference. During the six years—first in the Labour Government, and secondly as Leader of the Party—I have been in a kind of Dr Jekyll and Mr Hyde position. I have tried to speak for the Party, . . . and on each occasion when I have spoken for the Party . . . I tried honestly and straightforwardly to state the Party's position. My own position . . . has never shifted.

The Chief Whip is in general charge of the junior whips. He negotiates with the Government Chief Whip or Opposition Chief Whip (as the case may be) concerning the order of business on the floor. The Party follows the customary practice, when there is a Labour Government, of appointing the Chief Whip to the salaried post of Parliamentary Secretary to the Treasury. The junior whips are assigned responsibilities for particular groups of Members. There were four junior whips in the 1931-5 Parliament, and six (one the Deputy Chief Whip) in the House after the 1935 Election. Each Labour junior whip in a normal House has responsibility for twenty or thirty Members ; the grouping after 1935 was : Scottish, Welsh, Durham, Yorkshire (two), London and Home Counties. The main task of the junior whips is to check on the attendance of Labour Members, and to act as tellers at divisions.

To direct the business of the Parliamentary Party, there is a full-time Secretary and a small permanent Secretariat financed by the National Party organization. The Secretariat consists of the Secretary of the Parliamentary Party, one assistant, one messenger, and three shorthand typists. Expenditures of the Parliamentary

Party office in 1931 were £2,309, in 1932 they were £2,992. Recent reports have lumped Parliamentary Party salaries with those of the Central Office.

The Secretary, Mr H. Scott Lindsay, was appointed as Parliamentary Assistant in 1906, when the Parliamentary Party was formed, later assuming the title of Secretary. He is concerned with such routine work as drafting Bills and amendments, handling Party correspondence, and with the broader problems of harmonizing the work of the Parliamentary Party with the decisions of Party Conferences, the opinions of the Executive, and the declarations of the National Council of Labour.

D. Parliamentary Opposition : Futile and Fruitful

Throughout the life of the Parliament which sat from 1931 to 1935 the Opposition's role was futile and unreal. Not only was the Government's majority so large that its defeat was impossible, but Labour's appeal to public opinion through debates was poorly reported in the newspapers and over the wireless, and even such reports as were made normally attracted little attention. Discipline in Parliament is growing increasingly strict ; nearly every vote is designated a vote of confidence by the Government ; only a handful of Members with personal followings in their constituencies dare to vote in opposition to their Party. Labour's best opportunity, as the Opposition, to carry its message to the country is through Party meetings, leaflet propaganda, and the limited facilities of the Press.

If, as a leading student of British legislation has suggested, " the main function of the Opposition is to prepare itself to take office ",[8] then the Labour Party between 1931 and 1935 was in a difficult position to carry out its essential duty.   The personnel of the group remaining after the landslide of 1931 contained only a handful of M.P.s with Government experience, while about one-half were miners' representatives who varied widely in ability and outlook.   The leadership of George Lansbury during these difficult years has merited praise from both sides of the House.

Sir Stafford Cripps contributed brilliance and great legal knowledge to the Parliamentary Party's work of opposition.   C. R. Attlee made good use of his wide governmental experience and his ability for clear thinking. Josiah Wedgwood, a Member of the Cabinet of 1924, remained in the House, but his individualist tendencies rendered his contribution to the Labour team rather small.   Arthur Greenwood won the Wakefield division in a by-election in April 1932, and was thereafter able to bear a large share of the Labour burden in the House.   The election of Arthur Henderson in the Clay Cross by-election of August 1933, greatly augmented the prestige of the Parliamentary Party, especially in the international field.   Dr Christopher Addison, who made a conspicuous success as Minister of Agriculture in the second Labour Government, won Swindon in a by-election during October 1934, and was able to assume leadership in various fields in the remaining year of the first National Government.

It must not be assumed that the rank and file Labour Members of the House did not carry their share.   They rose to the occasion and, armed with briefs and material from the Labour Party Research Department, made admirable presentations of Party policy in fields which were completely new to them.   By the force of necessity, miners became experts in farming ;   an intellectual exposed alleged fallacies in certain military legislation.   The attendance of the Labour Members was exceptionally regular ;   one report showed that from November 3rd, 1931, to November 17th, 1932, eighty-five per cent. of the Labour Members voted on half or more of the divisions, while for the same period only fifty-seven per cent. of the Conservatives voted.[9]

In Opposition, the Party makes its chief case against Government Bills during the second reading debate on the principles of the proposed legislation.   Both the opening and closing Labour speakers are designated officially by the Parliamentary Party ;   others must obtain recognition from the Speaker for themselves. To most Government Bills, on second reading, the Party moves a " reasoned " amendment which is worded like a motion of censure, often beginning, " That this House regrets the failure of His Majesty's Government to recognize the urgent necessity . . ." Where the Government, as since 1931, has a large majority there is, of course, little chance that such a motion will be adopted.

During the committee stage, which follows second reading, the Party generally submits detailed amendments, and, in rare cases, secures their adoption with the aid of Government supporters. Increasing use has been made of this device in recent years, and the support of powerful organized groups is often obtained for the amendments. The Labour Members of Parliament use extensively their opportunity to make enquiries of Ministers at question time ; facts brought out by questioning doubtless have a considerable effect on Government policy.

Labour Bills are introduced and sometimes advance to second reading before the nearly inevitable defeat or emasculation by the majority. Measures like the recent holiday with pay Bill are used to focus public attention on the Government's refusal and Labour's willingness to act.

E. Labour Representation in the House of Lords

The representation of the Labour Party in the House of Lords has increased steadily in recent years, but it is still far from proportionate to Labour strength in the House of Commons or in the whole electorate. Of the 742 peers in the House of Lords in October 1935, only 16 were members of the Labour group, an increase of 4 since 1931. Eight of the peerages held by Socialists were created during Labour Governments, the other eight are hereditary or were created by other Governments. The most prominent of the latter are : Lord Parmoor, who was " elevated " by a Liberal Government in 1914, and Earl (Bertrand) Russell, who succeeded to his brother's title in 1932. In addition Dr Christopher Addison recently has been sent to the

House of Lords on one of the National Government's honours lists.

The two peers created by the 1924 Government, Lord (Sydney) Olivier and Lord (Sydney) Arnold, are becoming less and less active in the House. Most of the work has been taken over by Lords appointed by the second Labour Government—especially by Lord Ponsonby, Leader of the Opposition in the House of Lords from 1931 to 1935 ; Lord Marley, Opposition Whip ; Lord Noel-Buxton, former Minister of Agriculture ; Lord Sanderson, former principal of Ruskin College at Oxford ; and Lord Snell, present Leader and also Chairman of the London County Council. Lord Addison's name now should be added to this list of active Labour peers, as should that of the Earl of Listowel, now assistant whip and a member of the L.C.C. Since the ancient title of Lord Strabolgi was inherited in 1934 by Commander Joseph M. Kenworthy, an energetic Labourite, the Labour peers have had the aid of that colourful figure. Lord Passfield (Sidney Webb) has attended the House of Lords infrequently since 1931. Webb, Strabolgi, Addison, Noel-Buxton, Ponsonby, and Snell previously had been prominent Labour Members of the House of Commons.

The smallness of the Labour group places a heavy burden of parliamentary work on the shoulders of the half-dozen active Labour peers. In order to present the Labour view in the second chamber, they must attend its sessions regularly and, more important still, do a large amount of preparatory work. Recognizing the impossibility of carrying the Labour proposals, the

Labour Lords make their fight at the second reading stage, but do not offer detailed committee amendments.

In 1932 the Labour group decided to abstain from voting as a Party against the second reading of Government Bills, on the grounds that the House of Lords has no right " to contest the considered decision of the House of Commons ". The text of the Labour statement was as follows :[10]

We, in the Opposition on these Benches, do not consider that Your Lordships' House, with its indefensible constitution, should be in a position to reject the measures introduced by a Government which has the support of a majority in the House of Commons of elected representatives of the people. When the Labour Government were in office we expressed very strongly this view, because the unrepresentative majority in Your Lordships' House could, and indeed did, reject measures passed by a representative majority in another place.

A Vote given against the Second Reading of this measure is at the same time a Vote in favour of the principle that Your Lordships' House have the right and are justified in rejecting a Bill passed by a majority in the House of Commons. Whatever we may think of the methods by which that majority was obtained, we do not regard it as the function of this House to contest the considered decision of the House of Commons. While, therefore, reserving to ourselves the right to vote on Amendments to Bills or on Motions which may be brought forward in this House, we shall abstain from voting as a Party against the Second Reading of Government measures which are sent up to us from another place.

The Socialist peers take a full part in the Lords' committee work ; one accepts election to the deputy-speakership of the House. Debate from the Labour

benches in the House of Lords is of a high standard,
and attendance of the Labour Lords is much better
than the average for the whole House.   There are
nearly always six or eight Labour peers in attendance
at House sessions.   Professor Laski's investigation of
the period 1919-31 disclosed that an average of only
eighty-three peers voted in divisions of the House of
Lords.[11]   The Labour case is presented to the Lords in
a temperate manner in keeping with the traditions of
the House.   Once during 1934 the Labour peers forced
an all night sitting on the " Incitement to Disaffection "
Bill, thereby breaking records of long standing.

A curious situation confronts the Labour peers.   A
Labour Party majority in the House of Commons
probably will lead to the abolition or further dis-
memberment of the second chamber.   The task of a
Labour Lord is to fill in until the great day arrives.
To some extent, past Labour Governments have used
the second chamber much as aldermanic seats on local
authorities, to bring into public service persons who
have special skill in particular fields, and do not choose
to run for the House of Commons.   Nearly all the men
sent to the peerage by the Labour Party have been
financially   independent,   thereby   eliminating   the
necessity of their earning a living by serving as directors
of business corporations in search of respectable names.

F.   THE SOCIETY OF LABOUR CANDIDATES

The Society of Labour Candidates is composed of
Labour Members of Parliament and other Labour
parliamentary candidates.   Its objects are (1) to

12

provide an agency through which candidates may meet one another and the Party leaders ; (2) to bring the candidates into touch with the Executive and the Central Office ; (3) to make the special knowledge of candidates available to others and to provide for the interchange of speakers and information ; all these, of course, serve the ultimate purpose of strengthening the Party by bringing better informed Members to Parliament.[12]

The first object is probably the most important. By their meeting of one another, candidates may develop an *esprit de corps*, and interests which reach beyond the boundaries of their own constituencies to the Labour Movement as a whole. Contact with the Party leaders keeps candidates informed on the parliamentary application of Party policy. While the second Labour Government was in office, the Society arranged regular meetings at the House of Commons, which were addressed by Ministers on the work of their departments.[13] Candidates thereby obtained the views of Government leaders, which they were able to take back and interpret to their constituencies.

Since 1931 the Society has continued to hold regular meetings at the House of Commons, featuring addresses on current problems by Party leaders and others.

The second aim of the Society, to provide an organized contact with the Executive and Head Office, is carried out through a joint committee representative of the Society and the Executive. This liaison committee has been concerned with problems of constituency organization and the application of Party policy. The

Society itself studiously avoids making any policy pronouncements. It is concerned rather with determining the proper interpretation and application to Conference policy declarations. Under the joint auspices of the Executive and the Society, successful conferences of candidates were held during 1935, 1936 and 1937 ; they were devoted to the consideration of organizational and policy problems.

The Society's third object, to provide for the interchange of ideas and information is accomplished, not only through meetings, but also through the medium of the Society's organ, the *Labour Candidate*, a four-page leaflet publication which is issued nearly every month. It contains articles and editorials on many phases of Party programme and machinery. Like the Society, the *Labour Candidate* is financed by subscriptions of the members. For 1932 the Society had 147 members and a total budget of nearly £75 ; for 1933 it had 183 members and £67.

CHAPTER EIGHT

REFERENCES

[1] Philip Viscount Snowden, *An Autobiography*, Vol. ii (London, 1934), p. 762.

[2] R. Bassett, *The Essentials of Parliamentary Democracy* (London, 1935), p. 186.

[3] *Labour Year Book*, 1916, p. 318.

[4] *Ibid.*, 1925, p. 151.

[5] *Ibid.*, 1926, p. 156.

[6] Walter H. Ayles, M.P., " What is the Matter with the Labour Party ? A Loyal Backbencher's Point of View ", *Forward*, August 22nd, 1931.

[7] *1935 Conference*, pp. 175-6.

[8] W. Ivor Jennings, " The Technique of Opposition ", *Political Quarterly*, Vol. vi (April-June 1935), pp. 208-21.

[9] *Labour Bulletin*, April 1935, p. 613.

[10] *1933 Conference*, p. 89.

[11] H. J. Laski and J. Crighton, " Some Notes on the House of Lords ", *New Statesman and Nation*, Vol. v (March 4th, 1933), pp. 245-6.

[12] " Constitution and Rules ", *Labour Candidate*, January 1933.

[13] J. W. Bowen, " Aims and Objects of the Society of Labour Candidates ", *Labour Candidate*, September 1932.

THE GENERAL ELECTION OF 1935 AND LABOUR'S ELECTORAL POSITION

A. PUBLIC OPINION AND THE INTERNATIONAL CRISIS

THE campaign for the General Election of 1935 was conducted in the midst of a major international crisis. This situation was most advantageous to the National Government and the *status quo*, for the British electorate demonstrated both in 1924 and in 1931 that it prefers the Conservative Party in critical times. In 1935, the Government enjoyed the additional advantage of having adjusted its foreign policy in line with the sentiment of the great majority of the electorate, as revealed by the National Declaration on the League of Nations and Armaments, popularly known as the " Peace Ballot ".

The Peace Ballot was an attempt to hold a national referendum on the broad issues of peace and disarmament.[1] Originally sponsored by the League of Nations Union, the ballot was conducted with the co-operation of political parties, churches, women's groups, and other national organizations. Both the Liberal Party and the Labour Party participated, but the Conservative Party declined to take part. The isolationist press alleged that the ballot was a weapon against the National Government. The canvass was carried on between November 1934 and June 1935, and over eleven million votes were secured.

The questions submitted in the Peace Ballot and the votes cast on each were as follows :²

1. " Should Great Britain remain a Member of the League of Nations?" Yes, 11,090,387 ; No, 355,883.
2. " Are you in favour of an all-round reduction of armaments by international agreement ? " Yes, 10,470,489 ; No, 862,775.
3. " Are you in favour of the all-round abolition of national military and naval aircraft by national agreement ? " Yes, 9,533,558 ; No, 1,689,786.
4. " Should the manufacture and sale of armaments for private profit be prohibited by international agreement ? " Yes, 10,417,329 ; No, 775,415.
5. " Do you consider that, if a nation insists on attacking another, the other nations should combine to compel it to stop by
    (a) economic and non-military measures ? Yes, 10,027,608 ; No, 635,074.
    (b) if necessary, military measures ? " Yes, 6,784,368 ; No, 2,351,981.

The results of the poll were overwhelmingly in favour of the League and the collective security system. Even before the canvass was completed, the National Government began to revise its attitude toward the League of Nations.

The Cabinet changes of June 7th, 1935, obviously were in preparation for a General Election. Next to the replacement of Mr Ramsay MacDonald by Mr Baldwin as Prime Minister, Sir Samuel Hoare's succession of Sir John Simon at the Foreign Office was perhaps most important. During Sir John's term as

Foreign Secretary, the British Government failed to support League action against Japanese aggression in Manchuria, and contributed to the failure of the Disarmament Conference.

Sir Samuel Hoare reversed the British policy toward the League in his speech at Geneva, in September 1935, when he declared that Britain would support collective action against the aggressor nation in the Italo-Abyssinian dispute. This action met with widespread approval throughout the country, but placed the Liberal Party and Labour Party in a difficult and vulnerable position. In the crisis, their most convincing indictment of the Government was its failure to support the collective security system. Although both declared themselves the original and dependable exponents of the League system, their protests did not convince a majority of the electorate. In addition, the Labour Party was seriously weakened by an internal crisis over the issue, as a result of which both George Lansbury and Lord Ponsonby resigned their posts as Leaders in their respective Houses, and Sir Stafford Cripps resigned from the Party Executive. Both Lansbury and Ponsonby acted as pacifists, who oppose military action under any circumstances. Sir Stafford contended that a system of collective security maintained by the force of imperialist powers did not merit the support of honest Socialists.

B.   Selecting a Date for the Election

The Parliament Act of 1911 requires that a General Election must be held at least once every five years.

Circumstances made it advantageous for the National Government, elected in 1931, to go to the electorate before 1936. First, the Royal Jubilee Celebration, commemorating the twenty-five year reign of King George V, was held in the summer of 1935 and aroused patriotic and imperial sentiments which definitely were favourable to Conservatism.

A second important element was the fact that economic conditions in Britain improved steadily after 1932. The Board of Trade production index for the first six months of 1935 showed that activity in every industry except mining and textiles was above the 1924 level, and all except mining exceeded the 1930 level. A real boom was recorded in the building industry. Employment was definitely on the increase, and except for a half-dozen distressed areas, there was comparative prosperity. Naturally the Government wished to hold an Election while it could claim credit for the economic improvement.

A third reason why the Government might have forced an autumn Election was the possibility, discovered in 1931, of embarrassing the Labour Party by making it fight a municipal and a General Election at about the same time. Not only does Labour place great emphasis on local elections, but many of the Party's best workers and Agents hold municipal offices. If the two campaigns must be fought by local Labour Parties in rapid succession, naturally the second suffers from the lack of money and the near impossibility of making two complete canvasses within a single fortnight or month.

The fourth factor favouring a 1935 Election was the heavy expenditure that had been incurred for propaganda and advertising by the Conservative Central Office throughout the summer and autumn. Since early summer, billboards were filled with National Government posters. Labour Agents reported in April that eleven talking-film vans were on the road with speeches and records of what the Government had accomplished. It would seem, therefore, that considerable financial pressure indicated an early Election.

Recognizing that the international situation gave the Government a winning issue, Mr Baldwin announced to the House of Commons on October 23rd that the dissolution would take place immediately, and that the Election would be held on November 14th. He pointed out the difficulties in holding an Election except in the autumn or during the first six weeks of the New Year. Financial business occupies the Government's attention during the spring and summer, while a December Election would interfere with the Christmas trade, and August and September would conflict with summer vacations. Then he claimed to choose November over January because there appeared to be a " lull " in foreign affairs for a few weeks, and because it was impossible to predict what the international situation would be after the first of the year. From the Conservative strategist's point of view, the real danger clearly was that the international crisis would pass, weakening the Government's appeal.

C. The Government's Campaign

In the campaign, the Conservatives asked for support of the National Government on its record of leadership in the League sanctions movement, and because of the improved economic conditions since 1931. On the League issue, the Government scored heavily, for Liberals and Labourites, finding themselves in agreement with Tory policy, were forced to resort to criticizing the past record of the Cabinet in League matters. The Conservatives asked for a mandate for an extensive rearmament programme. On the domestic side, the Government made a strong case out of the economic recovery which Britain has experienced since 1931—building activity, improved export trade, and increased home markets. A modest programme of social reform was promised. The Tory attack on the Opposition was confined largely to " scare " publicity on various phases of the socialization plans of the Labour Party, chiefly banking, and to stress on the unpreparedness of Labour to assume power. The following titles to Tory leaflets indicate the nature of the " scare " propaganda : " Chaos and Crisis ", " Leaders at Loggerheads ", " Guard Your Savings ", " Your House to Go ! Your Building Society Too ! If Socialism Comes ", " The Socialist Policy Means War ", " Some Costs of Socialism ".

The Government used most advantageously the radio time allocated to it by the British Broadcasting Corporation. Five broadcasts were granted to the Government, four to the Labour Party, and three to the Liberal Party. Government speakers were

Mr Baldwin twice, Mr Ramsay MacDonald, Sir John Simon, and Mr Neville Chamberlain.

All parties to the Coalition worked together harmoniously. Unlike the campaign of 1931, there were no conflicting candidatures of National Government supporters. The Liberal Nationals pressed the point of the value of team play within the Coalition, and concentrated their attack on the official Liberal programme. They received full Tory support in the constituencies which they contested. National Labour similarly appealed for support of the Government, generally placing its candidates where they had clear fields against official Labour.

D. Campaigns of the Opposition Parties

Jockeyed into a most difficult position, the Labour Party approached the Election without confidence in its chances of winning a majority. Throughout the campaign Labour made its strongest case against the Government's rearmament programme.

It attacked the past foreign policy of the Government, alleging that British unfaithfulness to international obligations had wrecked the Disarmament Conference and had permitted Japanese aggression in China. Domestically, the Party criticized the increased cost of living, championed the contemporary demands of the coal miners for higher wages, and attacked the policy of reducing unemployed benefits, particularly the Government's " means test ".

The Labourites had difficulty in counteracting the record of the last Labour Government, which was regarded by large sectors of the electorate as a failure. Mr Attlee carried his new work·as Leader reasonably well, but was unable to offset the damage done to the Party's chances by Mr Lansbury's resignation. The impression of a considerable proportion of the voters, that the Labour Party leadership was divided, proved very damaging at the polls.

The Labour Party's wireless broadcasts were badly handled. Attlee, Clynes, Greenwood, and Morrison were selected for the four broadcasts allocated to the Party ; none made outstanding presentations of the Labour case. The omission of Lansbury was a costly error, for it emphasized the seriousness of the internal troubles, and deprived the Party of one of its most popular and effective speakers. Two of the three Liberal radio speakers, Lloyd George and Lord Snowden, urged the electors to choose either Opposition Liberals or Labourites.

The Liberal Party, clinging to its historical aims of social justice and peace, campaigned quietly and without much effectiveness. Chief interest centred in the activities of the Council of Action, promoted by Lloyd George and others, which offered its programme of peace and reconstruction to candidates of all Parties. Endorsements were given to all who answered satis-factorily three questions : the first required acceptance of the Council of Action policy ; the second called for a pledge to join an inter-Party parliamentary group to promote its policy ; the third asked for a pledge to carry out the policy even should the Government refuse it.

The Council's peace policy called for full acceptance of the League Covenant, collective action to end Italian aggression, an arms truce and non-aggression pacts for five years, a Conference of Kellogg Pact signatories, and settlement of grievances of dissatisfied powers. Its reconstruction " New Deal " involved a large public works programme, reciprocal tariffs, assistance to agriculture, an economic planning agency, extension of health insurance, raising of the school leaving age, and provision of retirement pensions. A total of 362 candidates from all Parties accepted the Council of Action policy ; 16 were supporters of the Government, 161 Liberals, and 183 Labourites. Although endorsed candidates obtained a total of 4,804,373 votes, only 67 were elected.

The Independent Labour Party, led by James Maxton, campaigned vigorously. All of the sixteen constituencies contested by the Independent Labour Party had a Labour candidate also, a situation which resulted in at least two mutual losses.   In accordance with the new policy of the Third International, the Communist Party supported Labour candidates in every constituency except two, where revolutionary sentiment was deemed sufficiently advanced to justify Communists.

The British Union of Fascists, although much in evidence, decided against entering the campaign, probably because Sir Oswald Mosley chose not to reveal the strength or weakness of his organization. Their advertised slogan for the election was " Blackshirts watch this futile farce and say ' Fascism Next Time.' "

E. Results of the Election

The National Government suffered a net loss of 83 seats, but remained with the overwhelming number of 431, of which 387 were held by Conservatives, 33 by Liberal Nationals, 8 by National Labour, and 3 by Nationals. The Opposition made a net gain of 83 seats, having elected 184 Members to the House of Commons, of whom 154 were Labour, 21 were Liberal, 4 were Independent Labour Party, 1 was Communist, 2 were Independent, and 2 were Irish Nationalists who have abstained from taking the oath or attending.

A comparison of the popular votes and the seats obtained by the various Parties after the last three Elections follows :[3]

	1929		1931		1935	
Party	Vote	Seats	Vote	Seats	Vote	Seats
Conservative	8,656,473	260	11,926,537	471	10,498,310	387
Liberal National	—	—	809,102	35	866,624	33
National Labour	—	—	343,353	13	339,811	8
Labour	8,389,512	287	6,648,023	52	8,326,131	154
Liberals	5,308,510	60	1,511,208	37	1,443,112	21
Others	293,880	8	421,181	7	527,849	12

It took an average of about 27,000 votes to elect a Tory, 54,000 to elect a Labourite, and 81,000 to elect a Liberal, reducing somewhat the absurd disproportion of the 1931 Election. Agitation for proportional representation arose again, but Labour continues to refuse support to a plan which may later prevent it from obtaining a clear majority in Parliament. If the seats had been distributed in proportion to popular vote, the Government majority would have been about fifty.

The reduction of the number of three-cornered contests accounts in part for the apparent paradox that Labour regained only about one-half of the 287 seats won in 1929, although its popular vote was almost equal to that year. A further loss of Labour seats and popular votes was due to the disaffiliation of the Independent Labour Party after the 1931 Election.

One of the most spectacular features of the contest was Labour's defeat of both Ramsay MacDonald, Lord President of the Council, and his son Malcolm, Secretary of State for the Colonies. National Labour candidates received rough treatment during the campaign at the hands of hostile audiences. Both MacDonalds won seats at subsequent by-elections : the father obtained a Scottish Universities seat ; the son won Ross and Cromarty in Scotland. Sir John Simon, Leader of the Liberal Nationals, narrowly avoided defeat.

Most of the Labour ex-Ministers who offered themselves for election were returned to the House, but Miss Margaret Bondfield, former Minister of Labour, W. Adamson, ex-Secretary of State for Scotland, Wedgwood Benn, 1929-31 Secretary of State for India, and Dr Christopher Addison, former Minister of Agriculture, were defeated. The Liberals fared badly at the polls ; Sir Herbert Samuel, Sir Walter Rea, Sir Robert Hamilton, and Mr Isaac Foot, all former Ministers, were defeated ; forty Liberal candidates lost their deposits ; the number of Opposition

Liberals in the House was decreased from thirty-four to twenty-one.

The Election left the Labour Party strengthened in the House of Commons ; the front bench was improved and augmented, and the total Labour seats more than trebled over 1931. The age level of the Labour group is very high ; Professor Laski reported in the *New Statesman and Nation* that only two Members are under thirty and only eight under forty. Among the Labour Party group there were seventy-seven Trade Unionists (including thirty-four miners, ten railwaymen, seven transport workers, six general workers, six distributive workers), twelve business men, eight Co-operative officials, eight barristers, eight teachers, five journalists, and five political officials.

Given the conditions under which the campaign was fought, the Labour Party did reasonably well at the polls. The Conservative scheme worked to perfection. Government strategists probably estimated sentiment in the country with a fair degree of accuracy by studying by-election returns. Labour's eleven by-election victories in 1933 and 1934 indicated that dissatisfaction with the Government was general, while 1935 by-elections, except for one freak result due to a Conservative split, demonstrated an apparent return to normalcy.

Not only did the National Coalition steal the Labour and Liberal peace thunder by supporting League sanctions against Italy, but it managed to hold the Election during a major crisis. Besides the usual advantages which the Conservatives enjoy over Labour (financial resources, normal majority in country), they had an additional trump card, namely Stanley Baldwin was dramatized successfully as the man " you can trust ", and the Labour Party virtually was Leaderless. The incidence of the municipal election a fortnight before the General Election was an added disadvantage. The rainy Election day also benefited the Tories, who usually can produce automobiles to carry voters to the polls.

F.   GEOGRAPHICAL DISTRIBUTION OF LABOUR PARTY STRENGTH

The 1935 Election re-emphasized the difficulties which the Labour Party must overcome to win a clear majority of all constituencies in the United Kingdom. The 154 seats held by the Party after the 1935 Election were less than half the number necessary to give it power.   In order to form a majority Government, Labour must win not less than all the constituencies which were carried in 1929, plus all others in which it came within 5,000 votes of winning in 1935 (excluding university seats).   If this could be achieved, and the present seats retained, the Labour Party would have a bare majority with 317 seats.

Its present strong position in London must be extended ; nearly eighty more seats must be won in the large English County Boroughs, especially in Birmingham, Liverpool, and Manchester ; representation in the industrial English Counties must be nearly doubled ; ten more Welsh constituencies must return Labour Members ; Scotland must be even more solidly for the

Labour Party than in 1929 ; the I.L.P. must return to the Labour Party. The distribution of the 317 constituencies which the Labour Party appears most likely to win may be shown as follows :[4]

CLASSIFICATION OF THE PARLIAMENTARY SEATS, SHOWING THE GREATEST LABOUR PARTY STRENGTH

Class of Constituency	Number of Seats	Total Necessary for Commons Majority	Seats won in 1929 or 1935	Never won, but within 5,000 votes in 1935
Total	615	317	292	25
London	62	41	38	3
English Boroughs	193	129	122	7
English Counties	230	77	69	8
Welsh Boroughs	11	10	10	—
Welsh Counties	24	18	15	3
Scottish Burghs	33	23	20	3
Scottish Counties	38	19	18	1
Northern Ireland	12	—	—	—
Universities	12	—	—	—

The Party has good prospects in London, where it has a strong local organization and controls a majority of the local government units. Labour strength in Wales is on the increase, and there is a good possibility that the quota of seats could be won. Scotland has always been a Labour stronghold ; reconciliation with the Independent Labour Party and the continuation of the intensive work in the Highlands probably will win the requisite number of Scottish seats. The bulk of seats must be won in English County Boroughs and Counties, where Labour did very poorly in 1935, though carrying all except fifteen of the required seats in 1929.

There, then, the Party must concentrate its efforts. Birmingham's twelve constituencies were all won by

Conservatives in 1935, partially due, it often is claimed, to the demoralizing effects of Sir Oswald Mosley's large expenditures on Party organization there between 1927 and 1931. The two key areas, from the Central Office point of view, may well be Lancashire and the West Riding of Yorkshire, both industrial areas in which Labour has lost much ground. Northern Ireland is so obviously and permanently Tory that contests there are likely to continue fruitless. Labour is making rapid progress in the rural areas of England, and there are a few in which it now appears to have chance of winning seats. The railroad and other transport workers carry the gospel of organized Labour to the farm servants, who sometimes still are regarded as sort of feudal subjects of the landowners. A strong Labour minority vote in the agricultural constituencies would be of great moral value in a crisis, and some County constituencies once regarded as " backward areas " may return before long Labour Members of Parliament.

G. Local Parties in the General Election

No description of Labour's part in a General Election is complete without an account of the basic work done in the local Parties. The transformation of Party units during campaign is roughly comparable to the changes made in an army during mobilization for action. In preparing for an Election, great stress is placed on the functioning of the polling district organization, whereas in normal times the activity of Party units rarely extends below the ward groups.

Take for examination a composite English provincial County Borough of 500,000, which is divided into six parliamentary constituencies. The Borough Labour Party is active ; the Trade Union official who is its Honorary Secretary manages to devote most of his time to Party work during campaigns. For the 1935 campaign, an " Election Fighting Fund " with a goal of £1,000 was launched by the Central Party ; the £600 actually collected was used for allocation to the Constituency Parties, for printing special leaflets and posters, and for arranging a mass demonstration featuring two national leaders during the final week of the campaign.

A hypothetical representative constituency within the same Borough was won by Labour in 1929, but lost in 1931. It is divided into four wards, each of which elects four Municipal Councillors, and each ward includes six polling districts. The Constituency Labour Party has an individual membership of about 2,000 ; more than two-thirds of the division is distinctly of the manual labouring class, but one ward contains a large number of white collar workers. The 1935 Official Register listed the names of 60,000 voters ; the Party's records showed that about 15,000 Trade Unionists and 20,000 Co-operative members resided in the constituency. The candidate, a London barrister, was selected by the Party in 1932.

About one month before the Election, the candidate announced the appointment of the full-time local Party Secretary and Organizer as his statutory Election Agent, and notified the " Returning Officer ". One of the first tasks of the Agent was to secure the signatures of numerous influential persons on the nominating papers of the candidate.   Then he set about perfecting the Party organization for the test.   He began with an internal canvass of the Party membership, conducted by the ward leaders.   Polling district secretaries then assigned Election canvassing responsibilities and obtained the promises of Party members to do campaign work.

By all odds the most important part of the campaign was the thorough canvass, by Party workers, of all voters in the division.   The general canvass is not, however, a feature of every constituency campaign. Many divisions which are securely Labour are never canvassed ; no canvass was made in 1935 in either George Lansbury's Bow and Bromley or in several of the Welsh mining constituencies.   On the other hand, constituencies where Labour is poorly organized are often not canvassed because there are not enough willing Party workers to conduct this rather bothersome work.

The canvassers were provided with the latest voting register, arranged by streets ; working in pairs, they distributed Party literature and ascertained how each voter intended to cast his ballot.   This information was recorded on a card provided by the Party, and turned in to the polling district secretary.   When the canvass was completed, the cards were sorted into " for ", " against ", and " doubtful " ; the cards of persons opposed to the Labour candidate were put aside ; those marked " for " were saved for Election day ; all " doubtful " were re-canvassed carefully. Complete records of the day to day status of the canvass were kept in each polling district, and a daily progress report sent through the ward leader to the Constituency Party committee rooms.

Second in importance in the campaign were the various ward meetings addressed by the candidate and his supporters. The candidate, occasionally with outside " big noises ", was scheduled to speak twice each evening. These meetings were carefully advertised by handbills and posters, which were distributed through the ward organizations and the League of Youth branch. Near Election day, the candidate, equipped with a mobile public address system, ventured into the streets of the constituency. Sometimes he participated in a " mass canvass ", in which Party workers rang door bells on a certain street, handed out campaign literature, and announced to householders that the candidate would speak on the corner within a few minutes. At other times a " progress canvass " was made, in which the candidate's visit was speeded up, and he remained only long enough to be seen and to answer a few questions. The candidate spent noon hours visiting factory workers at their lunch.

In the meantime, activity in the Party office reached a feverish pace. A dozen Party workers were busy addressing envelopes which were to carry the candidate's " Election Address " and the " poll card " to each voter in the division ; the Post Office allows each candidate one post-free Election communication per voter. A clerk was occupied with checking out leaflets and posters to a ward leader. The Party's publicity manager was putting the final touches on an Election "news sheet", a four-page tabloid size newspaper, giving details about the candidate and the Labour Party programme. Working behind a collection box, was the financial secretary, who was later able to report that an election fund of £300 was raised from individual subscriptions and the collections which were a ritual at every meeting.

On the eve of the poll, rallies were held at eight points in the division; the candidate managed to devote about ten minutes to each. Younger Party workers placed a final message of the candidate on the doorstep of every voter the night before Election. At each polling place, a Party "personation agent" served as the poll watcher, while a "runner" with a conspicuous red ribbon in his lapel collected the poll cards of Labour supporters after they voted. The poll card, giving the address of the polling place, is issued by the Party and carries an "X" by the name of the Party candidate. Voters are under no compulsion to hand these cards to Party workers, but generally do in order to avoid being canvassed again. In a rough way, the number of Party cards collected indicates the number of votes cast for the Party candidate. These were taken to the polling district secretaries, who maintained up-to-the-hour records of who had voted. Every effort was made to get Labour voters to the polls, but the Party was greatly handicapped by its lack of motor cars, especially during the closing hour.

The candidate managed to win by a majority of about a thousand, a much smaller margin than in 1929, but some improvement over 1931. He lost a part of the vote of factory workers in the engineering trades because the Government promised that its rearmament programme would give them continuous employment. A number of unemployed were frightened by the National candidate's warning that a Labour victory might bring a financial crisis with a resulting reduction of the dole. The candidate was continually embarrassed by the Communists, who offered to assist in the campaign ; but heresy hunters within his own Party strongly opposed accepting their help, and his Conservative opponent watched carefully for an opening to pin the radical label on him. A major blow was the loss of a large portion of the peace vote—the free church people, the League of Nations Union members, and the ex-Liberals who usually voted Labour ; many of these people were won over by the Government's strong action in support of the League.

CHAPTER NINE

REFERENCES

[1] Dame Adelaide Livingstone, *The Peace Ballot, The Official History* (London, 1935), p. 5.

[2] *Ibid.*, pp. 9-10, 34, and supplementary sheet facing p. 34.

[3] The Election statistics used are those of *The Times House of Commons, 1935* (London, 1935).

[4] Computed from Election statistics in *The Times House of Commons, 1935* (London, 1935).

THE LABOUR PARTY AND LOCAL GOVERNMENT

A. LABOUR'S INTEREST IN MUNICIPAL POLITICS

LOCAL government has been regarded by many as a primary concern of the Labour Party, ranking in importance with the Party's work in Parliament. " Indeed ", Mr Herbert Morrison has written, " it is perhaps true to say that up to the present Labour's most creative work has been in the field of local government administration."[1]

The reasons for the Party's participation in municipal affairs include the following : (1) municipal campaigns offer a means of building up popular support and perfecting the Party machine in periods between parliamentary Elections ; (2) local councils afford a training ground for Labour political leadership ; (3) municipalities provide laboratories for experimentation with socialized services ; (4) Labour control assures local co-operation with the socialization plans of a future Labour Government ; and (5) Socialist local authorities may, through the social services, alleviate some of the suffering and distress of the working class.

Throughout most of the Party's history, however, its leaders have devoted their attention almost exclusively to national affairs, often neglecting the municipal field. William A. Robson was able to declare after the second Labour Government, that the Movement had " scarcely begun to think constructively on the subject of local government. . . ."[2] In two terms of office, the Party enacted only two important pieces of municipal legislation, both housing Acts.

Moreover, the second Labour Government failed to support the " Local Authorities (Enabling) Bill ", which the Party had pushed when in Opposition, and to which it was pledged in *Labour and the Nation*, the official statement of aims. The Bill would have granted general powers to larger municipalities to conduct " trading " enterprises. It was brought before the Commons as a private Bill by Labourites, but was opposed by Mr Greenwood, Minister of Health. It must not be assumed, however, that all Labour leaders have overlooked the importance of the municipal field, for some of the present front benchers have made important contributions to local government. Mr Attlee is author of a number of works on local government ; Mr Morrison has devoted years to building Labour strength in London ; Mr Lansbury furnished spectacular leadership to his Metropolitan Borough Council. Mr Robson, the Webbs, Mr Cole, and others have contributed significantly.

The Labour Party lacks a definite and comprehensive municipal programme. Local government received little attention in *Labour and the Nation*, the 1928 statement of policy and programme, and even less in *For Socialism and Peace*, adopted in 1934. Early Party

declarations stressed the necessity of giving municipalities a free hand to develop local services and " for
adequate local control ".[3] Recent statements, both
official and by individual Party leaders, reveal a
growing tendency toward centralization. The Party's
housing policy stated in *For Socialism and Peace*
contemplates a national agency for slum clearance
and rebuilding where municipalities are unable or
unwilling to carry out the central programme.

The present Leader of the Party, in discussing
problems of the Socialist transition, has proposed the
creation of regional authorities, appointed by and
responsible to the central government, with control
over local authorities in each area. His case for this
action was made in the following statement :[4]

Although for normal times I support the British tradition
of local government, I consider that in a period of critical
transition when society is undergoing fundamental change,
it is essential that there should be available in each locality
an administrative machine which will be energized and
controlled by the Central Government.

After the Socialist system has been established, Attlee
would have local authorities resume their powers and
carry on their normal functions. It is clearly recognized
by many Socialists that Labour's advent to power
nationally, may lead to less, not more, municipal home
rule.

B.   British Municipal Structure

Of the sixty-two Administrative Counties in England
and Wales, Labour has been able to capture, and now

holds, only four—London, Durham, Monmouth, and Glamorgan. The County Councils have important powers over education, public health, roads and bridges, public assistance, police, and planning. Their jurisdiction over local affairs is shared, however, with Urban and Rural District Councils which have limited authority over sanitation, housing and planning, public health, roads, and, in the case of the former, elementary education in districts with a population of 20,000 in 1901.

Also within the area of the Counties are the Municipal Boroughs, with Councils of slightly more power than Urban District Councils. County Councils have no jurisdiction, however, over eighty-three larger cities, called County Boroughs. These are governed by Councils under broad grants of power that are roughly equivalent to the aggregate of those delegated to Counties and their subdivisions. Labour has held majorities on twenty-one County Borough Councils, and nineteen Municipal Borough Councils.

London government adds to the complexity ; the Administrative County of London contains twenty-eight Metropolitan Boroughs and the ancient City of London, each with its Council of less authority than those of County Boroughs, though more than those of Municipal Boroughs. Metropolitan Borough Councils have limited jurisdiction over public health, housing and slum clearance, streets, libraries, public baths, and in some cases electricity.[5] The Labour Party has held, and now holds, a majority in seventeen of the twenty-eight Metropolitan Borough Councils.

C. Extent of Labour Success in Local Elections

The growth of the Labour Party and its entry into municipal politics inaugurated a new era of Party strife in British local affairs. The early activities of the Independent Labour Party and the Labour Party frequently led to Liberal-Conservative coalitions against the " Socialist threat ". Scattering seats on County and Borough Councils were won before the war, but the real gains followed 1918. Labour steadily increased her strength up to the elections of 1930, lost heavily in 1931, then proceeded to rise to a new record in 1934 ; in 1936 another decline was registered. The trend of Labour's electoral progress in municipal government may be ascertained from the record of the Party's net gains of seats in English and Welsh County Borough and Municipal Borough Councils :[6]

Elections	Labour's Net Gains	Elections	Labour's Net Gains
1923	69	1930	− 73
1924	53	1931	−238
1925	75	1932	22
1926	148	1933	250
1927	114	1934	305
1928	127	1935	30
1929	219	1936	− 48

The Party's record in Metropolitan Borough Council elections has been less gradual because the elections are held only once every three years. The number of majorities won by the Labour Party in the last six elections for the twenty-eight London Borough Councils may be shown as follows :

Elections	Number of Labour Majorities	Elections	Number of Labour Majorities
1919	13	1928	8
1922	6	1931	4
1925	8	1934	15
		1937	17

It is obvious that Party successes in municipal elections closely follow public sentiment as revealed at General Elections, in spite of the fact that the electorate and the problems are considerably different. The local franchise is denied all except owners or tenants of property with a rateable value of ten pounds annually, or the wife or husband of such an owner. This property qualification, disadvantageous to Labour, is probably balanced by the superior ability of the Socialist forces to get out their vote.

Briefly, Labour's status on the chief English and Welsh local authorities as given in the latest *Local Government Speakers' Handbook* was :

	Total Number	Labour Controlled
Counties	62	4
County Boroughs	83	21
Metropolitan Boroughs	28	15 (now 17)
Other Boroughs	289	19

D. LIMITATIONS ON LABOUR MUNICIPAL ACTION

British local government is limited to powers specifically granted by statute. If British municipalities enjoyed " home rule " in the older German sense, experimentation with municipal socialism might be carried out by the Labour majorities on local authorities. But the general laws rigidly restrict municipalities to specific functions, and local Acts are not easy to obtain through the slow and costly private Bill procedure in Parliament. Therefore Labour Boroughs and Counties have been confined to the conventional and undramatic task of running the existing municipal machinery, making minor achievements by increasing relief, providing more school meals, or expanding a health service.

Even within the limits of statutory authority, however, British municipalities are not free, but are checked by central administrative supervision.[7] The powers of control exercised by the Ministry of Health include : authority to issue rules and orders ; to approve the by-laws, schemes, and loans of local authorities ; to hear appeals in a quasi-judicial capacity ; to act in default of local authorities ; to inspect local services ; to control extension of functions ; to appoint District Auditors ; to control grants-in-aid.[8] The Board of Education has wide powers over local educational authorities ; the Home Office has a growing control over local police ; recent developments have increased the authority of the Ministry of Transport over roads and highways.

In two previous long terms of Conservative rule in the central government, 1925-9 and 1931-5, there has been tension between Labour municipalities and the supervising agencies. During the first period, central authority was strengthened by the House of Lords' decision in the Poplar Wage Case, confirming the power of a District Auditor to hold local expenditures "unreasonable" and to surcharge individual Councillors for excess amounts paid.

The Poplar Borough Council had carried out the principle of "model employer" to the extent of establishing a minimum weekly wage of four pounds. This was not objected to by the District Auditor at the time, but in 1923 he ruled that the minimum was excessive, disallowed the amount paid in excess of standard trade agreements, and surcharged the Councillors. On appeal his decision was reversed by the Court of Appeals, but the House of Lords upheld the Auditor and the Councillors were surcharged. Soon thereafter the Audit (Local Authorities) Act of 1927 enacted that persons surcharged over £500 were disqualified from holding municipal office for five years.

Under the Local Government Act of 1929, the Minister of Health was given authority to reduce the grant-in-aid to any authority which failed to achieve and maintain a reasonable standard of efficiency in public health, or was making excessive and unreasonable expenditures.[9] The Minister of Transport was given similar power over road grants. In this period, the Minister of Health also acquired the power to supersede poor relief authorities if their relief scales are deemed too generous.

Examples of these controls which operate to curb the activities of Labour-controlled municipal councils are numerous. In 1932 the Board of Education demanded that teachers' salaries be cut to the full extent authorized by administrative order, threatening to estimate the excess of those salaries and reduce the grant-in-aid accordingly. The Minister of Health in 1934 denied the application of Leeds for permission to start a scheme to sell furniture to tenants of municipal houses. Durham County Councillors were surcharged £950 for excessive expense accounts paid to the County Accountant.

The greatest controversy arose over the administration of the " Means " test for transitional benefits to persons passing from unemployment insurance to public assistance. A large number of Labour Councils refused to administer the test, which was regarded as offensively invasive on private affairs. They were superseded by special commissioners appointed by the Minister of Labour. At some point in nearly every phase of its activity in providing model public health services, the Bermondsey Metropolitan Borough, for example, has been forced by central authorities to delay or change its plans for the expansion of municipal services.

The municipalities which have come under Labour control have a number of common characteristics. The typical Borough or County with a Labour majority on its Council is primarily industrial, with a working class population, a serious unemployment problem, and a heavy relief burden. The three Counties where Labour has held power for some time—Durham, Glamorgan, and Monmouth—all are in special distressed areas where industry and mining are in a particularly serious condition. In September 1935 the percentage of unemployment in relation to the insured population in these counties was thirty-four, thirty-seven, and thirty-four respectively, as compared with an average of sixteen for Great Britain as a whole.[10]

In October 1935 the seventeen Labour-controlled County Boroughs for which figures are available had seven per cent. of their aggregate population out of work ; for all England and Wales the average was four per cent.[11] About two-thirds of London's unemployed in January 1935 were grouped in the fifteen Metropolitan Boroughs on the Councils of which Labour had a majority. Large numbers of those out of work have been unemployed for long periods, and have passed from unemployment insurance benefits to public assistance, which is still a local charge.

The plight of Labour municipalities in general is further intensified by the fact that their assessed valuation is extremely low. Every County Borough under Labour control in 1932-3 had a rateable value *per capita* below the average for England and Wales ; one had a value of one-half the average.[12] Only one of the fifteen Labour Metropolitan Boroughs had a *per capita* rateable value as high as the average for the whole County of London.[13] The combination of a low assessed valuation and a heavy relief burden results in a high tax rate. Every Labour County Borough had a rate above the 1932-3 national average of thirteen shillings and one penny to the pound of rateable value. Merthyr Tydfil had a rate of twenty-seven shillings and sixpence, making the tax actually due on property in the Borough more than one hundred per cent. of the assessed rateable value! All except one of the London Boroughs with Labour majorities in 1934-35 had tax rates above the County average.

E. WHAT LABOUR DOES IN MUNICIPAL OFFICE

Although the Labour Party lacks a general defined municipal programme, the Councils which it captures act along certain predictable lines. Public assistance benefits are generally more liberal in Labour municipalities ; this fact is demonstrated clearly in the following comparison of relief standards :[14]

AVERAGE SCALES OF RELIEF REPORTED TO THE ROYAL COMMISSION ON UNEMPLOYMENT INSURANCE, 1931

	Man and Wife.	Man, Wife, and 3 Children.
	s. d.	s. d.
Average for 65 County Boroughs	21 0	30 2
Average for 9 County Boroughs under Labour Control	22 11	32 4
Average for 17 Counties	20 1	27 8
Average for 3 Counties under Labour Control	23 8	31 6

Nearly every municipality which has come under Labour rule has expanded its public health facilities. Particular emphasis is usually given to maternity and child welfare work. The more extensive services provided by Labour County Boroughs in this field are shown in the following figures on attendances at clinics :[15]

ATTENDANCE AT COUNTY BOROUGH INFANT WELFARE CENTRES AND ANTE-NATAL CLINICS IN ENGLAND AND WALES, 1932, 1933, 1934

Percentage of Registered Live Births of :	1932		1933		1934	
	England and Wales	Ten Labour Boroughs	England and Wales	Six Labour Boroughs	England and Wales	Five Labour Boroughs
Children under one year attending first time	55·9	57·5	56·8	59·4	56·1	68·5
Women attending	37·6	42·6	41·1	48·1	42·4	38·1

There is also a significant tendency for Labour-controlled local authorities to provide a greater number and a more extensive array of educational services at a cost usually higher than the national average. Measured in cost per child, the higher educational expenditures of County Boroughs under Labour rule may be compared with the average cost in all County Boroughs as follows :[16]

THE COST PER CHILD OF ELEMENTARY EDUCATION IN COUNTY BOROUGHS, ENGLAND AND WALES, 1927-34

Average Cost per Child	1927-1928	1928-1929	1929-1930	1930-1931	1931-1932	1932-1933	1933-1934
	s.	s.	s.	s.	s.	s.	s.
All County Boroughs	230	245	251	259	248	239	241
Labour County Boroughs	239	252	259	268	260	269	287

Anti-Socialists claim that the higher expenditures of Labour-controlled local education authorities are due to inefficiency. Labourites answer that the greater education costs arise from the fact that they provide more school meals, a larger number of free places in secondary schools, and university scholarships. The Labour Party also has been very active in promoting a reduction in the size of school classes ; Labour-controlled municipalities, in many cases, were the last to reduce teachers' salaries, and the first to restore the cuts after economy sentiment had subsided.

Local Labour Councils have been able to do very little in extending the range of municipal trading services, chiefly because of the impossibility of securing parliamentary sanction. Nearly all have set up or extended municipal works departments in order to handle construction and repairing directly without the intervention of a contractor. Work performed on " direct labour " projects of Labour-controlled municipalities usually is performed under good conditions, with good wages and a more certain period of employment than private employers offer.[17] Several Labour Boroughs with municipal electricity and gas undertakings have reduced rates in hopes of increasing consumption.

Leeds, under Labour rule, in effect discriminated against its own electricity undertakings and in favour of a private gas company by refusing to install electricity for any purpose except lighting in municipal housing schemes. Glasgow, another Labour city, adopted the same practice as Leeds, thereby benefiting the private company which wholesales gas to the municipal distributing agency.[18]

Considering that Labour's experience in local government has been limited chiefly to the poorer areas which face the riddle, as G. D. H. Cole aptly expressed it : " The poorer the area, the greater the need ; the greater the need, the less the resources,"[19] the affairs of Labour-controlled municipalities are well administered. Almost without exception, Labour Council majorities have conducted municipal business with what is now regarded as the traditional British respect for clean government. As Bernard Shaw has pointed out, in *Essays in Fabian Socialism*, the fact that Labour Councillors are under close scrutiny by anti-Socialists makes them perform their duties more conscientiously. The record of the Labour Party in municipal government may be described in a sentence : in office, the Party does not, indeed cannot achieve socialism, but it is confined chiefly to spending more and providing more services.

F. PARTY ORGANIZATION ON MUNICIPAL COUNCILS

It is inevitable that occasional controversies should arise over the conduct of the business of the Labour groups on various municipal Councils. Numerous cases of procedure, discipline, and policy have been appealed to the National Executive. Inasmuch as the Executive considered there was a need for an outline of standard practice setting forth in detail the general organization of local authority Labour Parties, it had a sub-committee draft for the purpose some model standing orders, which were approved by the 1930 Conference.

According to the provisions of these standing orders, ordinary meetings of the group are held at an agreed time between the publication of the Council agenda and the meeting of the Council. Contact is maintained with the local Labour Party concerned by having three representatives attend Party meetings in a consultative capacity. Officers of the group, Chairman and Leader, Vice-Chairman and Deputy Leader, Chief Whip and junior whips, are elected by the group at its annual meeting. General executive work is conducted by a policy committee consisting either of Labour members of the Council's general purposes committee, or the officers and three members selected by the group.

Party policy on matters before the Council is determined by the full meeting of the group. Election policy is pronounced by the local Labour Party. In cases of emergency the policy committee or Leader may act, but must report at the next meeting. Labour members are required to vote with the majority decision of the group, except on certain matters of conscience, when they may abstain if they have raised the point in a previous meeting. Private motions by Labour members must be submitted to the group. Members are allowed freedom to ask questions in Council, unless they are deemed contrary to Party policy. All members must accept the standing orders, and if they are violated, the group whip is withdrawn after consultation with the local Labour Party. Such action is subject to a final appeal to the National Executive.

The same general principles are applied to Party organization on Council committees, and co-opted members are on the Party committee group. Professor Laski stated in *A Century of Municipal Progress* that there has been an "immense development of an informal (Party) committee system behind the legal structure". It is now general for Party groups to meet before the formal committee meetings, in order to review the agenda and decide on the Party attitude. This makes the regular committee meeting less a pooling of minds than a test of Party strength. The Labour group on the Council reports occasionally to local Parties.

Although these standing orders were drafted for local authorities outside of the Administrative County of London, much the same plan of organization is used by the Labour groups on Metropolitan Borough Councils. The organization and procedure on the London County Council follows the same general pattern, but is necessarily more elaborate ; a detailed description of it will be made below.

In general, the discipline imposed by the Labour Party groups on local authorities is rigid. There is a tendency to make group decisions on a very large proportion of council business. In his preface to E. D. Simon's *A City Council From Within*, the late Graham Wallas warned the Labour Councillor of the danger that the "strict caucus discipline which is traditional in his party" might prevent the necessary "intellectual elasticity" to secure success for a "large administrative policy".

Laski regrets the loss of the "independent member of goodwill" who serves as a public duty, and the tendency to make technical questions partisan ones. He welcomes, however, the fact that with partisan rivalry, policy becomes more coherent and local achievements are speeded up. After weighing both sides, he concludes that the "clarity of objective" under partisan system compensates for the losses.

Religion or temperance are the most common reasons given by conscientious objectors. The strictness of Party conduct is well illustrated in the case of Alderman Sir Percival Bower, former Lord Mayor of Birmingham, who was expelled from the Labour Party for disloyalty in May 1932. The culminating incident was his refusal to obey instructions of the group to vote against a motion to confer the freedom of the city on their fellow townsman, Mr Neville Chamberlain. Sir Percival was elected to the local Conservative Club the following year.

Labour groups generally follow the established local practice in the selection of Aldermen. In municipalities where Labour was given a proportionate number of Aldermanic appointments when the Party was in a minority, the same privilege has been given the Opposition after Labour won a majority. Where, as in Sheffield, the Municipal Reformers (Conservatives) when in power took all the Aldermanic seats, Labour, on getting a majority, adopted the policy of making only their own partisans Aldermen. The practice of appointing only elected Councillors to Aldermanic posts is looked upon with some disfavour in the Labour Movement because of the expense and risk of resulting by-elections. There is a growing sentiment that the device of appointing Aldermen should be used to strengthen the Party group on the

Council by adding specialists in certain phases of the Council work.

G. THE LONDON COUNTY COUNCIL LABOUR PARTY

The Administrative County of London exceeds in population and importance all other British municipalities, and the control of its governing body, the London County Council, has been regarded as of great strategic value to the Labour Party. The triennial election of all Councillors of the capital city offers the Party an opportunity of winning a spectacular victory. Although it shares the responsibility of local government with twenty-eight Metropolitan Borough Councils, the London County Council has great powers over education, housing, health, poor relief, public works, planning and other services which intimately affect the lives of Londoners. The great diversity of wealth between the various Boroughs provides the County Council a chance to collect taxes in rich districts and spend for social services in the poorer areas. Because each London division is one-half of a parliamentary constituency, the regular Party organization is readily adapted to municipal campaigning.

After its establishment, in 1888, the London County Council divided sharply along Party lines, and its partisanship has been carried to much greater lengths than in provincial municipalities.[20] Until 1907, the Progressives (Liberals) had an unbroken period of power, in which the tradition of clean and efficient government was firmly established. Sidney Webb, Ramsay MacDonald, and other Labour leaders, served on the Council as Progressives and played a leading role in the extension of educational, utility, and social services. During the long rule of the Municipal Reformers (Conservatives), 1907-34, the Labour members formed their independent group, gradually built up strength, became the official Opposition in 1925, and achieved a majority in 1934.

In Opposition for many years, the Labour members of the County Council made a vigorous fight against " Toryism ". The battle was not one against corruption, for the County government was and is regarded as an example of civic purity. It was a conflict, rather, between two fairly well defined philosophies. The Municipal Reformers sought to provide a minimum number of services at the lowest possible cost, and to avoid competition with private enterprise ; the Labourites, on the other hand, urged the extension of public services, and the advisability of municipal public service enterprises.

Up to 1934, Labour advocated additional educational facilities, a liberalized housing policy, more public health services, and improved public assistance administration. The Council Labour group devoted many years to the exposure of schemes, the alleged purpose of which was to hand over the County's public tramways system to the private bus and tube " combine ". All three transport services were nationalized in the London Transport Act, legislation originally drawn by Mr Herbert Morrison, Leader of the Labour group on the Council, while he was Minister of Transport, 1929 to 1931. At one time, the Party took a leading part in disclosing the unsuitable condition of public markets. After the advent of the National Government, the Labour minority fought the economy programme which the Government urged and the Conservative majority on the Council carried out.

In its struggle for supremacy in the London County Council, the London Labour Party enjoyed several advantages. A powerful local Party organization had been built up and maintained at a high standard of efficiency. Labour leadership both in the London Party and in the Council has been unusually stable. A recent study of the personnel of the London County Council revealed that Labour members compare favourably with Municipal Reformers in both formal higher education and extent of previous political experience.[21] The talents of Mr Morrison, who heads both the London Party organization and the County Council Labour Group, are conceded even by Labour's opponents.

The campaign for the election of March 8th, 1934, was fought on a number of comparatively minor issues ; Labour pressed its case for improved and increased housing, education and other services, and urged the need for liberalized public assistance administration ; the Municipal Reformers campaigned against extravagance and for economy.[22] The polling was light, and the landslide victory probably unexpected even by the leading Labourites ; Labour obtained sixty-nine seats to the Municipal Reformers' fifty-five, and in total votes, 341,390 to 298,464 ; the Liberals were completely eliminated. On the basis of official records of campaign expenses, the Labour Party spent about fivepence halfpenny per vote obtained ; the Municipal Reformers just over fourteen pence ; and the Liberals nearly twenty pence.

The 1937 election was fought mainly on Labour's record in office. Labour pointed with pride to its three years of action—especially the Party's aggressive re-housing policy, and more liberal administration of public assistance. The Municipal Reformers stressed achievements of their own long period in power, criticized the increase in rates since 1934, and condemned Communist electoral assistance to the Labour Party (which Mr Morrison likewise deplored). The election results were even more pro-Labour than those of 1934. The Party gained ten seats and lost four. Labour then had seventy-five Councillors to the Municipal Reformers' forty-nine. After the allocation of Aldermen, the division was eighty-seven for Labour to fifty-seven for Municipal Reform. Again the Liberals were left without a seat.

The seats won by the major Parties in the seven elections since the war are as follows :

Year	Labour	Municipal Reform	Liberal
1919	15	68	40
1922	16	82	26
1925	35	83	6
1928	42	77	5
1931	35	83	6
1934	69	55	0
1937	75	49	0

The Labour majority proceeded at once after the 1934 election to organize the new Council, choosing Lord Snell of Plumstead, a prominent Labour peer, as Chairman. In accordance with the established practice of the Council, the twenty Aldermanic seats were allocated between the Parties in proportion to their Councilmanic strength, and the chairmen and vice-chairmen of committees were drawn entirely from the majority Party. Mr Morrison, as Party Leader, assumed the important post and title of Leader of the Council, with functions somewhat comparable to those of the Prime Minister in Parliament. After the 1934 selection of Aldermen, Labour had a working majority of sixteen. After 1937 the majority was thirty.

In the London County Council Labour Party, the weekly or special meeting of all Labour Aldermen and Councillors is supreme. The policy committee, composed of Labour members of the general purposes committee of the Council, is an executive body similar in some respects to the Cabinet, for it includes nearly all the chairmen of committees. This group meets on days preceding a Council meeting, considers both matters referred to it by the full Party caucus and business brought to it from the Council committees through the Leader.

On the Council floor, the Party presents a united front against the Municipal Reform group, and its members vote in accordance with the Party decision made by the full caucus or the policy committee. A Chief Whip and three junior whips are responsible for attendance for getting their Party colleagues into the proper division lobby. Committee attendance is highly important, and members are often designated as committee whips. As in the House of Commons, there is a question time, during which the Opposition may ask the Leader or committee chairmen concerning County business.

There is a harmonious relationship between the political Council and the permanent administrative staff, whereby administrative officers may be called upon by committees or individual members of either Party for information regarding their departments, but avoid entirely Party controversies. On assuming office in 1934, Labour members of the new Council were reminded by Party leaders of the necessity of avoiding charges of influence and jobbery in appointments, and ordered never to approach an official on any matter of employment. The Party Leader similarly directed the administrators never to accept applications for employment through any Council member.

In the first three and a half years of Socialist rule, the London County Council has made numerous changes of policy and alterations of practices. In housing, the economy policy has been reversed, the clearance of all London slums scheduled, and rents for Council houses reduced. School rebuilding and repairing has been revived ; the number of scholarships and free places in secondary schools has been increased ; there has been a considerable extension of school meals and school health services ; expenditures for educational services generally have been pushed up. As expected, the Labour County Council administered public assistance more liberally, made numerous improvements in public hospitals, purchased new land for park purposes. Hours of work of County employees have been reduced, salary cuts restored, staffs increased, and conditions of work improved in a number of County departments.

All this has cost a great deal, but the Council determined to face the necessity of raising the tax rate at once, and proceeded to increase it by tenpence halfpenny to a new level of seven shillings in the pound of rateable value. It announced that this new rate would provide the revenue necessary for Labour's programme during the three year term of office. By this bold and immediate action, the Party leaders hoped both to avoid criticism for trying to conceal the increased tax burden and to give the electorate sufficient time to forget the increase. Their estimates of income, however, proved optimistic, and the Council was forced to raise the rates again in March 1936. Both of these increases were attributable in part to reduction in rateable value.

A number of conflicts with the National Government have taken place ; the most spectacular was over the rebuilding of Waterloo Bridge over the Thames, the reconditioning of which had been under discussion for ten years. After parliamentary aid was refused, the Minister of Transport rejected the County's application for a grant, so the Council began the demolition and reconstruction out of County funds. London

15

Labourites have cited this action as an example of their Party's decisiveness and speed. Subsequently, a settlement has been reached.

There are severe limitations on what the Labour majority on the London County Council can accomplish. Not only is the Council checked by the usual administrative supervision of the central Government, and restricted to specifically delegated powers, but the boundaries of the Administrative County are so far out of harmony with the actual extent of the metropolitan area that the County cannot deal adequately with the larger problems of Greater London. Only about one-half of the eight million population recorded by the census for Greater London (the Metropolitan Police District) live in the County of London. The remainder live in the rapidly growing " outer ring " in the Counties of Middlesex, Surrey, Kent, Essex and Herts, and are governed by a complexity of County Boroughs, Municipal Boroughs, Urban Districts, Rural Districts, and Parishes, which cover the area.

From this outside " dormitory " region a million or more workers daily come into the County of London to offices and factories ; they are provided with costly municipal services which are furnished by the County and the Metropolitan Boroughs. Because the big problems of London cover the whole metropolitan area, there is an increasing tendency to form special agencies and special districts to deal with particular problems ; the Metropolitan Water Board, the Metropolitan Police District, and the London Transport Board are results of this tendency.[23]

Within its sphere, the London County Council under Labour rule appears to have made a reasonably good record. By London's special position, the Party is precluded from obtaining any measure of municipal socialism, but it has gained something in popular confidence by administering London affairs with skill and efficiency, and has alleviated some suffering in the poorer districts by its more liberal policy in the social services. The basic issue before London electors in 1937 was—are the augmented services furnished by the Labour Council majority worth the extra money which they have cost ? The electorate's verdict was " Yes ".

CHAPTER TEN

REFERENCES

1 In forward to H. R. S. Phillpott, *Where Labour Rules : A Tour Through Towns and Counties* (London, 1934), p. v.

2 William A. Robson, " Valediction : A Frank Survey ", *Local Government News*, Vol. viii (December 1931), p. 78.

3 *Local Government Handbook,* issued by the Joint Research and Information Department of the Trades Union Congress and the Labour Party (London, 1924), pp. 220-2.

4 C. R. Attlee, " Local Government and the Socialist Plan ", in *Problems of a Socialist Government* (London, 1935), p. 191.

5 Mrs I. M. Bolton and Dr S. W. Jeger, *London's Borough Councils : Their Constitution : Their Powers : How They Do Their Work*, issued by the London Labour Party (London, 1934) ; C. R. Attlee, *Metropolitan Borough Councils : Their Constitution, Powers, and Duties*, Fabian Tract No. 190 (March 1920) ; Herbert Morrison, *How Greater London is Governed* (London, 1935), pp. 100-8.

6 *Local Government Speakers' Handbook*, 1937-8 Edition, p. 4.

7 See W. A. Robson, " The Central Domination of Local Government ", *Political Quarterly*, Vol. iv (January-March 1933), pp. 85-104 ; G. D. H. Cole, *The Future of Local Government* (London, 1921), pp. 3-7 ; C. R. Attlee and W. A. Robson, *The Town Councillor* (London, 1925), pp. 17-18 ; W. A. Robson, *The Development of Local Government* (London, 1931), pp. 337-53 ; W. A. Robson, *The District Auditor : An Old Menace in a New Guise*, Fabian Tract No. 206 (1923) ; W. A. Robson, *The Relations of Central and Local Government*, issued by the New Fabian Research Bureau, March 1933.

8 See W. Ivor Jennings, " Central Control ", in *A Century of Municipal Progress* (London, 1935), pp. 142-5.

9 *Ibid.*, p. 444.

10 See Ministry of Labour, Statistics Branch, *Local Unemployment Index*, No. 105 (September 1935), pp. 1-4.

11 Computed from *Ministry of Labour Gazette*, Vol. xliii (October 1935), p. 392.

12 Ministry of Health, *Annual Local Taxation Returns, England and Wales, 1932-3*, Part II (London, 1934).

13 London County Council, *Statistics of Metropolita Boroughs, 1934-5* (London, 1935), p. 7.

14 Computed from *Minutes of Evidence taken before the Royal Commission on Unemployment Insurance, Eighth Day*, Thursday, January 22nd, 1931 (London, 1931), pp. 299-304.

15 One Labour Borough, West Ham, is included in the totals, but omitted from the figure for Labour Boroughs because its attendances greatly exceed its registered births. West Ham clinics are well known and widely used by persons coming from East London and other areas outside the limits of the County Borough. Total infant welfare figures from : *Sixteenth Annual Report of the Minister of Health, 1934-5* (August 1935), pp. 291-337 ; figures for individual Labour Boroughs furnished by the Ministry of Health ; statistics on registered live births from : *The Registrar-General's Statistical Review of England and Wales for the Year 1932.* (New Annual Series, No. 12), Tables, Part I, Medical (London, 1933), Table 17 ; *Ibid., 1933* (No. 13), Table 17 ; *Ibid., 1934* (No. 14), Table 17.

16 Computed from statistics presented in *Board of Education, Elementary Education, England and Wales, Cost per Child Elementary Education Calculated upon the Actual Net Expenditures of Local Education Authorities in the Financial Years (April 1st to March 31st) 1931-2, 1932-3 and 1933-4*

Respectively (London, 1935) ; *Ibid., 1928-9, 1929-30 and 1930-1* (London, 1932) ; *Ibid., 1925-6, 1926-7 and 1927-8* (London, 1928). The greatly increased expenditures in Labour Boroughs during 1932-3 and 1933-4 may be due in part to the small sample. In the latter two years only seven County Boroughs were under Labour control.

[17] Labour Research Department, *Direct Building, A Study of Building by Direct Labour Under Local Authorities and the Practical Problems Arising* (London, 1929), p. 25 ; R. B. Suthers, *Mind Your Own Business, The Case for Municipal Housekeeping* (London, 1929), pp. 74-9.

[18] Political and Economic Planning, *Memorandum on Electricity Distribution*, January 14th, 1936, pp. 24-5.

[19] G. D. H. Cole, *The Next Ten Years of British Social and Economic Policy* (London, 1929), p. 314.

[20] Sir Harry Haward, *The London County Council from Within* (London, 1932), pp. 22-33.

[21] Eleanor Ernst, " The Personnel of the London County Council ", *Political Quarterly*, Vol. vi (July-September 1935), pp. 417-23. This survey covered the Councils of 1931-4 and 1934-7.

[22] W. A. Robson, " Thoughts on the L.C.C. Election : The Chaos of Local Government ", *Political Quarterly*, Vol. v (April-June 1934), p. 168.

[23] See Herbert Morrison, *How Greater London is Governed*, pp. 1-7 ; W. A. Robson, *Ibid.*, pp. 171-3 ; Herbert Morrison, "A New Era for London", *Labour*, Vol. i (May 1934), p. 196 ; " The L.C.C. Election ", *New Statesman and Nation*, Vol. xiii (February 6th, 1937), pp. 193-4.

PART IV
TACTICS AND POLICIES

DEFECTIONS AND PROPOSED ALLIANCES

SHARP differences of opinion have always existed within the Labour Party. A few have been so serious that minority groups have felt it necessary to leave the Party and pursue their objectives independently. From the early post-war period until the second Labour Government began to falter, however, there were no seceding groups of importance. Like those of other great political parties, Labour's programme was sufficiently general and its discipline lax enough that it could include persons with diverse political philosophies ranging from near-Communism to near-Toryism. The crisis of the second Labour Government, however, precipitated three secessions of importance : (1) Sir Oswald Mosley and a handful of followers, (2) Ramsay MacDonald and his National Labour Group, and (3) James Maxton and the Independent Labour Party. These three splits gave rise to extremist factions which became targets for especially vigorous Labour attacks.

A. SIR OSWALD MOSLEY AND THE BRITISH UNION OF FASCISTS

The Mosley split was least important from the point of view of losses to the Party, but the potentialities of the Fascist Movement which he now leads at times has caused more disquiet in the Labour Movement than either the MacDonaldite annex to the Conservative Party or the small Socialist faction in the Independent Labour Party. The rise of Oswald Mosley in Labour politics was meteoric. Entering the Party after some experience in the Conservative ranks, he won his spurs by hard work, strove for spectacular leadership, and used his private fortune to build up the Labour organization in the Birmingham constituencies. Rewarded with a minor post in the second Labour Government, Mosley set to work with characteristic energy at the task assigned to him, the framing of plans for dealing with unemployment. J. H. Thomas and Philip Snowden rejected nearly every suggestion he made, and the Cabinet gave him added rebuffs. Sir Oswald, therefore, resigned from the Government in May 1930, and immediately organized an appeal to the 1930 Conference to adopt the " Mosley Plan "— an elaborate scheme of public works—but was defeated by a narrow margin.

The next step in Mosley's career was the organizing of the " New Party " with John Strachey, Dr Robert Forgan, Lady Cynthia Mosley, all Labour Members of Parliament. Five Labour Members of Parliament resigned from the Parliamentary Party between February 24th and March 4th, 1931. Sir Oswald Mosley was expelled by the National Executive on March 10th. A Conservative Member of Parliament and a Liberal joined the group later. The group advocated the emergency programme drafted by Allan Young, Mosley's political secretary, John Strachey, and other Labour Members of Parliament. The programme called for recognition of the prevailing crisis, control of imports, national planning, delegated legislation, and works projects.[1]

The New Party had a short and troubled existence. When Mosley began to show Fascist tendencies, Strachey joined the Communist Party, and nearly all the Labour men returned to their former Party fold.[2] Mosley had boasted that the New Party would put a great number of candidates in the field at the next General Election, but when the 1931 campaign arrived, his Party had only eighteen candidates. Nearly all lost their deposits ; even Mosley made a poor showing in his wife's former constituency at Stoke-on-Trent.

Almost without followers, Sir Oswald Mosley, in pursuit of power and action, organized the British Union of Fascists in September 1932. Pouring his own money and ability into the Movement, Sir Oswald was able to carry on intensive propaganda, and to attract a considerable number of young men of the middle class. It has been estimated by the National Council of Labour that the Fascist membership was in 1934 not more than 20,000.

The British Union of Fascists programme has never been made clear. Mosley's book, *The Greater Britain*, is a rather muddled attempt to restate the Fascist doctrine in the light of British temperament. The State is glorified ; self-sufficiency of Empire is praised. Mosley would sweep away the hindrances involved in traditional parliamentary procedure, and substitute a dictatorship of action. The British Fascists seek power by the ballot box, but once Parliament is captured, the " organized obstruction of minorities who at present use Parliamentary procedure to frustrate the will of the nation " will be suppressed, and absolute power of action conferred on the Government.[3] Sir Oswald has defined fascism as " Leadership of the people with their willing consent along the path of action which they have long desired."[4]

Mosley's Fascists imitate the German Nazis and Italian Fascists by wearing distinctive shirts and forming themselves into a semi-military organization. Mosley rarely is mentioned by name, but is always called the " Leader ". Jew-baiting plays a prominent part in Fascist activities in East London, but in general the Movement did not stress it, until 1935 and after. British Fascist propaganda is continuous and apparently well financed ; leaflets, pamphlets, and books are issued in quantities ; two papers, *Action* and the *Blackshirt*, and a quarterly review are published ; meetings are held throughout the country ; many Fascist posters are on the bill boards, and slogans are written over walls and bridges.

The unpopularity of Hitler in Britain was intensified by the " blood purge " of 1934, and Mosley's forces suffered a consequent loss of prestige. In June 1934, attempts to break up a Fascist meeting at Olympia resulted in a riot in which blackshirts used allegedly brutal methods in ejecting disturbers, which were widely publicized in *The Fascists at Olympia*. The House of Commons debate on the episode was damaging to the British Union of Fascists. Mosley's Movement received a further set-back during the Italian-Abyssinian dispute, when feeling against Italian Fascism ran high.

Loss of the libel suit brought by Lord Camrose against the periodical *Action*, although imposing no impossible direct financial burden on the Fascist Movement, may prove a telling blow to blackshirt prestige. Fascist membership has declined markedly, according to recent reports, accentuated perhaps by the State ban on uniforms and paraphernalia imposed by the Public Order Act. The Movement remains in the public eye largely because of publicity received from leftish counter-demonstrations which usually accompany Fascist parades.

B. DEFECTION OF THE NATIONAL LABOUR GROUP

The crisis of August 1931, produced one of the most spectacular shifts in the history of British politics, when J. Ramsay MacDonald and a small group of followers left the Labour Party and joined the Coalition National Government. The cleavage between the main body of the Party and those who chose to go along with the Prime Minister was not the real dividing line between the Labour left and right, but rather a sloughing off of a certain section of the right, chiefly non-Trade Unionist, which had been in part influenced by factors of temperament and outlook. If the differences had been confined to the question of crisis strategy, National Labour participation in the National Government would have been brief, and the group's re-admission to the Party might have been possible. But MacDonald's compromising and fondness of Conservative social circles, Thomas's pleasure in elegant company, and Snowden's caustic criticism of his former colleagues rendered such reunion impossible, especially after the 1931 Election.

What then was the philosophy of the National Labour group ? Actually it had no programme beyond the emergency period. Individual MacDonaldites, seeking to justify their increasingly difficult position, have issued some statements of policy. The ablest of these was written by Clifford Allen (now Lord Allen of Hurtwood), the last " moderate " Chairman of the Independent Labour Party before Maxton and the " left " captured control. Allen made a strong case in justification of Mr MacDonald's action in August 1931, by showing that the Labour Cabinet admitted the seriousness of the crisis, considered retention of the gold standard to be imperative, yet refused to make the necessary economies demanded by those who could make the loans to save it. MacDonald, he claims, made the heroic decision not to leave the sinking ship, even though his comrades chose that course.[5] Lord Allen later turned to advocating a democratic coalition of the Liberals, moderate Labourites (mentioning especially Herbert Morrison, Philip Noel-Baker, Sir Walter Citrine, and Ernest Bevin), and a few progressive Conservatives.[6]

A second supporter of the MacDonald group was Godfrey Elton (now Lord Elton), a teacher in Oxford University and the author of *England Arise ! A Study of the Pioneering Days of the Labour Movement.* Elton's chief thesis was that the Labour Party is not a National Party, but rather a sectional faction condemned to be a permanent minority.[7] Although he condemned the Trade Unions for their demands for " succour for the working classes in the shape of cash benefits which overtaxed the resources and alienated the sympathies of the nation ",[8] he later suggested that Trade Unionists might obtain much more if they would bargain with various Parties rather than support the " permanent " Opposition.[9] Lord Elton has called the National Labour group a " political nucleus " around which will gravitate those Socialists and Trade Unionists " who in the coming years will turn instinctively from the wilderness into which they are being hounded ".[10] It is difficult to see how the group can exist other than dependent upon Tory charity.

Some attempt has been made by the National Labour group to keep up the pretence of a separate identity. A twopenny fortnightly, the *News Letter*, contains editorial comment and articles in support of the National Government, and some literary comments. It is not inspiring, is written from a rather defensive, apologetic point of view, and gives the impression that it is only marking time until something happens. Now that Ramsay MacDonald has passed from the scene, it appears inevitable that the survivors of the group will be assimilated finally into the Conservative Party. A similar fate probably awaits Sir John Simon's Liberal Nationals.

Outward evidence of the coming change is found

in Malcolm MacDonald's decision to fight the Ross and Cromarty by-election in February 1936 as a " National " without the " Labour " suffix. The censure of J. H. Thomas by the tribunal which conducted the budget disclosure inquiry of 1936 and his subsequent retirement was a considerable blow on the prestige of the group.[11] Sir William Jowitt, former Attorney-General in the National Government, has been re-admitted to the Labour Party and endorsed as a parliamentary candidate. Of the important National Labourites, only Malcolm MacDonald remains in the National Government. His problem of maintaining both " face " and office is a difficult one.

C. The Disaffiliation of the Independent Labour Party

The Independent Labour Party played an historical role of great importance in the building of the Labour Party. In the early period it was the agitation of the I.L.P. which led to the formation of the Labour Representation Committee ; it was partially the I.L.P. which was responsible for the Labour Party's acceptance of Socialism in the programme of 1918. But the constitutional changes of that year provided also for an individual membership, and took from the I.L.P. its important task of recruiting non-Trade Unionists for the Labour Movement.

The I.L.P. continued to be active and virile for several years thereafter ; but with the termination of the first Labour Government the old leaders drifted out of their I.L.P. offices and were replaced by younger " left " Socialists. In 1926 James Maxton became chairman, and the organization began, as a German observer aptly put it, " to rocket aimlessly in space ".[12] Philip Snowden and other older leaders resigned from the I.L.P., and the group experienced a slump in membership.

While the I.L.P. was " rocketing " with schemes to cure the various ills of the world, the Labour Party successfully fought the Election of 1929 and formed the second Labour Government with Liberal support. To maintain this minority Government, it was necessary for the Party to enforce rigid discipline in the House of Commons. The I.L.P. protested in 1930 that Members should not be asked always to vote with the Government, and declared that the I.L.P. could not accept new limitations on the obligations which its Members of Parliament owed to constituents and to socialism.[13] After the 1930 Conference, the I.L.P. withheld its endorsement from all candidates who refused to sign a group pledge. Only fourteen of the 142 Members of Parliament who then belonged to the I.L.P. agreed to accept these conditions.

Maxton declared, with much justice, that the acceptance of all Cabinet proposals was unreasonable when the Parliamentary Party was not consulted and, he alleged, " in many instances do not comply with the programme authorized by the Labour Party Conference ".[14] Mr A. Fenner Brockway, Chairman of the I.L.P., in the *New Leader* during 1931, indicated three cases where the Government had disregarded decisions reached in Party meetings and had acted contrarily.

He also listed 122 Labour Members of Parliament who had voted against the Government on different occasions.

All through this period, regional I.L.P. meetings and local branches were discussing the question of disaffiliation from the Labour Party. A statement of the situation was issued by the I.L.P. National Council in June 1931, in which the central issue between the I.L.P. and the Labour Party was described as the difference between real " Socialism in Our Time " and " short view policies of maintaining the Government ". A month later the I.L.P. Members of Parliament refused to accept the Labour Party Standing Orders, and the die was finally cast by the decision of the Labour Party Conference to refuse endorsement to any candidates who refused to accept the Standing Orders of the Parliamentary Labour Party. Of twenty-two candidates who refused to accept the Standing Orders, six were elected ; only one was opposed by an official Labour candidate. This group was not invited to the Parliamentary Labour Party meeting, and was recognized by the Speaker as a separate political Party.

A controversy within the I.L.P. raged over the proposed disaffiliation.[15] The case for unconditional affiliation was ably presented by the late E. F. Wise, " left " Labour Member of Parliament (1929-31) and adviser to the " Centrosoyus ", the Russian consumers' co-operative union, who maintained that the I.L.P. could not hope to make the Labour Party more Socialist by leaving it, nor could the I.L.P. alone ever gain sufficient strength to form a Government. H. N. Brailsford argued that the I.L.P.'s job was to educate and organize from within, for it would be " ridiculous if it were not painful, that our tiny group should stand apart when a mere remnant of a Labour Party faces overwhelming hosts ".

Six I.L.P. regional Conferences in January 1932 considered the question ; five favoured continued affiliation and only one, London and South, supported withdrawal. Although Maxton, Brockway and other influential leaders supported disaffiliation, the regular I.L.P. Conference at Easter, 1932, defeated a resolution in favour of leaving the Labour Party by a vote of 183 to 144 ; but unconditional affiliation was rejected also, and a resolution for conditional affiliation was adopted, 250 to 53.[16]

The conditions under which affiliation was to continue required that another attempt be made to reconcile the differences with the Labour Party. Consultations and correspondence over a two-months period were resumed. On June 1st the Parliamentary Labour Party decided not to revise its Standing Orders but agreed to review the question before the next Labour Government was formed. The Labour Party National Executive, later in the month, adopted a resolution that the Standing Orders of the Parliamentary Party were primarily its own concern, and that the I.L.P. Members of Parliament should join the Parliamentary Labour Party if they wished to secure amendment of Standing Orders.

Thereupon, the I.L.P. called a Special National Conference at Bradford on July 30th, 1932, to which

the National Council recommended immediate disaffiliation. Among the delegates were three rather
distinct groups : (1) moderate disaffiliationists, led by
Maxton, Brockway, and the I.L.P.'s Members of
Parliament, lined up a majority of votes for immediate
disaffiliation and in support of a rather muddled
statement of policy and new Constitution ; (2) revolutionary disaffiliationists, led by Dr C. K. Cullen,
mustered small support for their policy resolutions,
which appeared near-communist ; (3) affiliationists,
led by P. J. Dollan and E. F. Wise, polled over one-
third of the votes against withdrawal. The first two
groups voted together for the disaffiliation resolution
241 to 142, but the moderate vote was large enough to
defeat all revolutionary proposals.[17]

These three groups have since gone three different
directions. The moderate disaffiliationists remain in
control of the I.L.P., which is weakened in membership
and dangles precariously between Moscow and Smith
Square. The revolutionaries left the I.L.P. on the
eve of the 1935 Election and joined the Communist
Party. The affiliationists resigned from the I.L.P. and
took with them a good proportion of the I.L.P. branches
and membership ; the Scottish affiliationists were
organized by Pat Dollan and Tom Johnston into the
Scottish Socialist Party ; some English and Welsh
affiliationists were reunited into the Socialist League.

In the course of the Bradford Conference of 1932, it
was stated both by Brockway and Maxton that the
policy conflict between the I.L.P. and the Labour Party
was more important than that over Standing Orders.

The enforcement of Party discipline demonstrated the lack of a " community of belief ", and since a " reasonable " degree of liberty was not permitted, the I.L.P.'s position became intolerable. What then was the chief basis of this conflict over philosophy ? There is no major point of difference between the objectives and programme adopted by the I.L.P. Special Conference or subsequent Conferences and that adopted by the Labour Party in *For Socialism and Peace*.

The only important divergence between the two lies in method ; but here the difference is chiefly one of stress.[18] The I.L.P. has chosen to talk in revolutionary terms, to speak of wresting control of the economic system from the hands of the capitalists, and to predict the inevitability of a crisis which will sweep the united working class to power. But its differences with the Labour Party were certainly no more fundamental than the Socialist League's quarrel with the official Party programme from 1932 to 1937.

The basic differences were in temperament. Maxton, outstanding leader of the I.L.P., is a born agitator, who by his nature finds greatest satisfaction in the minority. As Professor Laski has written, Maxton's job is to arouse emotion, and this he does with " complete artistry ".[19] Maxton's laudatory biography of Lenin reveals his own indecision over whether or not man must " proceed by way of struggle, violence and brute force ".[20] Perhaps the most serious loss to the Labour Party in the disaffiliation of the I.L.P. was the loss of Maxton, who is one of the most colourful of British Socialists.

Since disaffiliation, the I.L.P. has pursued a rather erratic course. The 1932 Bradford Conference decided that both individuals and branches of the I.L.P. must disaffiliate from the Labour Party ; I.L.P. members of local authorities must leave the Labour groups and form separate groups ; individual Trade Unionists in the I.L.P. must cease to pay the political levy. It has been charged that the discipline imposed by the I.L.P. became far more strict than that ever required by the Labour Party.

When political levy exemption forms were distributed by the I.L.P. among Trade Unionists, a storm of protest was aroused, and Trade Union leaders made devastating attacks on this " organization of place seekers and political blacklegs ".[21] The I.L.P. was forced to retreat and cancelled its instructions regarding the political levy, explaining that the Unions had barred from all political discussions I.L.P. members who refused to contribute. Total I.L.P. membership dropped to 15,000, about one-half the pre-disaffiliation level ; expenditures were so drastically curtailed that the Head Office budget was cut to nearly one-fourth. The I.L.P. is strongest in Scotland ; all of the four I.L.P. Members of Parliament came from Glasgow constituencies. Of seventeen I.L.P. candidates in 1935, eight lost their deposits.

Once free of the Labour Party, the I.L.P. began negotiations with the Communist Party and the Third International, seeking a " united front " and discussing the possibility of I.L.P. affiliation to the Communist International. The 1934 I.L.P. Conference decided against affiliation with the Third International. The I.L.P. withdrew from the Labour and Socialist International and has been co-operating with the International Bureau of Independent Revolutionary Socialist Parties, which is made up of its prototypes in other countries.

Co-operation with the British Communist Party has been only slightly successful. The National Council was able to report to the 1935 Conference that they had " reached agreement on common action on specific objects " with the Communist Party.[22] Some joint agitations and demonstrations against war and fascism, against the attacks on the unemployed, and in support of oppressed Spanish and Austrian workers were organized. Such common endeavours practically ceased after the change of tactics ordered by the Communist International in 1935, under which the British Communist Party supported most Labour Party candidates. Disgusted, the I.L.P. turned to attacking the Communists as counter-revolutionary !

The I.L.P. itself has been weakened further by internal splits. The late R. C. Wallhead, one of the most popular men in the Labour Movement, resigned from the I.L.P. following its 1933 Conference, and applied for re-admission to the Parliamentary Labour Party. He resigned because the I.L.P. Conference chose to rank revolutionary action before political action, and re-entered the Labour Party because he was " profoundly impressed " by the spread of fascism in Europe and the need for a united working class. David Kirkwood, a Glasgow Member of Parliament who left the Labour Party with the I.L.P. group, applied for the Labour whip in September 1932. Both were welcomed back to the Parliamentary Labour Party.

The group split-off of the revolutionary disaffiliationists has been mentioned already in this section. In January 1932 this group organized itself into an informal and unofficial "revolutionary policy committee" within the I.L.P. The committee had two aims : first, to win the I.L.P. away from reformism and towards revolution, involving disaffiliation from the Labour Party ; and second, to lead the I.L.P. to negotiate for affiliation with the Communist International.[23] The first objective was achieved at least in part ; the I.L.P. did disaffiliate, and gave lip service to revolutionary phraseology. But the revolutionary group met uncompromising opposition to its proposals for affiliation with the Third International.[24] When the group joined the Communist Party in October 1935, its announced reasons were chiefly the " disruptionist " tactics of the I.L.P. The I.L.P., it was charged, (1) refused to aid in the necessary fight to displace the National Government, (2) failed to support the collective security system of the League of Nations and misrepresented the foreign policy of the Soviet Union, (3) distorted the objectives, tactics, and policy of the Communist International and championed another international which further divided the forces of socialism.[25] According to Dr Cullen, chief spokesman of the group and suitably enough, a physician, the I.L.P. " lives each day in a world of yesterday, and borrowed, and out-of-date slogans are its staple article of diet ". It is widely believed within the I.L.P. that some of the revolutionary group were Communist " contacts " instructed by the Communist Party to remain and bore from within ; the I.L.P. claims that only sixty-three members left with the group to join the Communist Party.

Few I.L.P. disaffiliationists, except the revolutionary group, had a definite idea where independence would lead them. Their position has remained indecisive. Because some I.L.P. Members of Parliament have personal followings in their constituencies, the group has persisted in the House of Commons. United action with the Communist Party is more and more out of the question as the full significance of Communist policy of supporting the Labour Party becomes clear. The I.L.P. continues to dangle precariously ; its leaders might agree to a federation relationship with the Labour Party if I.L.P. M.P.s could have a considerable degree of freedom, but the Labour Party continues to repeat George Lansbury's invitation, " Welcome back on the same terms and conditions as we apply to ourselves."

D. RELATIONS WITH THE COMMUNIST PARTY

" The clear line that divides the Communist and Socialist movements was drawn later in Great Britain than in any other country in Central or Western Europe," wrote Wertheimer in 1929. The reasons for this are to be found both in the tolerance of the British and in the federal nature of the Labour Party under which Trade Unionists were automatically members of the Party. From its formation in 1920, the Communist Party adopted a policy of permeation and infiltration into the Labour Party. The Labour Party Conference of 1920 first rejected the Communist Party's application for affiliation. Similar applications were turned down in 1924 and 1925. Nevertheless, leading Communists continued to represent Trade Unions and local Labour Parties at the Labour Conferences, and some were even elected to office as Labour candidates. The 1924 Conference took the first step toward ejecting the Communist element by declaring members of the Communist Party ineligible for endorsement as Labour candidates to any public office and, by a close vote, barring Communists from individual membership in the Labour Party. Communist Trade Unionists, however, continued to come as delegates to the Party Conferences.

The 1928 Conference built the barrier even higher by providing : (1) that affiliation with the Labour Party implies loyalty to Conference decisions and debars affiliates from promoting candidates opposing those of the Labour Party ; (2) that neither candidates who opposed Labourites nor members of political Parties ineligible to affiliation (Communists) could be delegates to National or local Party Conferences or meetings ; (3) that local Parties must allow only those who advocate Labour principles and policy to speak at public meetings. But the tactics of the Communist Party were already being altered in accordance with new directions from the Communist International.

British Communists opposed the proposal of the Third International executive committee, which ordered them to pursue independent political action and fight the Labour Party, but the International's decision was accepted by a Communist Conference early in 1929.

For six years the British Communists pursued their extremist policy without tangible results. Attacks on the Trade Unions and the Labour Party, especially after 1931, accomplished little except to increase the workers' hostility toward their noisy attempts to disrupt the Movement.

A new era of Communist Party activity began in mid-1935, with the alteration of policy made by the seventh Congress of the Communist International. This new tactical line called for co-operation of the various Communist Parties in the development of a broad united front against war and fascism ; in Britain it involved the union of " left " forces to defeat the National Government and to set up a Labour Government. The able Secretary of the British Communist Party, Harry Pollitt, put the case for the new tactics in these words :[26]

> The overwhelming majority of the masses of this country who are organized in the co-operatives, the Labour Party, and the Trade Unions are still under the influence of the Labour Party. It is not Maxton they see, it is not Baldwin they see, it is not Pollitt they see, it is the Labour Party they see, and the possibilities of a Labour government, and the sooner we recognize that the better.

For purposes of the new " unity ", the Communists offered to withdraw a " considerable number " of their candidates if Labour would allow a clear field to a few Communist candidates. Although the Labour Party declined to make such an agreement, the Communists entered only two candidates, both in constituencies where there was a minimum chance that splitting the working class vote would result in victory for a common enemy. In Rhondda East, a South Wales mining constituency, Pollitt stood alone against a Labour candidate, but lost by more than 8,000 votes ; in West Fife, a Scottish mining division, Willie Gallacher won by a plurality over W. Adamson, a former Labour Cabinet Member, and a Conservative candidate. Throughout the rest of the country the Communists aided Labour candidates, and their assistance probably was praised as much as damned by Labour candidates and Agents.

After the Election the Communist Party again applied to the Labour Party Executive for affiliation, and the Socialist League supported the application. In Parliament, Gallacher made conciliatory speeches and applied for the whip of the Parliamentary Labour Party. This was impossible under the Constitution of the Party, but he has continued to work in harmony with the Labour group. The Executive again turned down the Communist application for affiliation, in January 1936. Both the 1936 and 1937 Conferences rejected proposals for Communist affiliation or unity.

It was over the issue of the " United Front " that the Socialist League was expelled from the Labour Party by the Executive in January 1937. The " Unity Manifesto " issued by the Socialist League, the

Communist Party, and the I.L.P. projected a rather moderate scheme of reform not widely different from Labour's Short Programme. Fortunately for the Labour Movement, the Executive's drastic action did not cause the withdrawal from the Party of Cripps, Laski, Brailsford, and other vital leaders of the " left ", but rather led to dissolution of the Socialist League. Apparently Cripps and Laski now intend to abandon their part in the unity campaign and to serve the Labour Party as members of the Executive Committee.

E. The Liberal Party and the Labour Party

The mind of Britain, a prominent Liberal peer wrote recently, is " still irredeemably Liberal ".[27]   If this is true, query his Labour critics, how is the poor showing of the Liberal Party at the polls to be accounted for ? The once great Liberal Party has been reduced to a condition in which its candidates in the 1935 Election received less than one and a half million votes, only twenty-one secured election, forty lost their deposits, and its official leaders were all defeated.   A wing of the Party has all but lost its identity in the present Coalition Government.   Mr Lloyd George, the most prominent Liberal now remaining in the House of Commons, was moved in 1933 to comment : " I see no future except a dishonourable grave for Liberalism as it is. Liberalism is in an advanced state of creeping paralysis."[28]

After the Liberal leaders resigned their Government posts in September 1932, and especially after November 1933, when the Liberals crossed the House to join the

Opposition, there was some discussion of a Liberal-Labour alliance to defeat Conservatism. Both the *Manchester Guardian* and the *News Chronicle*, chief Liberal newspapers, urged the necessity of an agreement with the Labour Party. The *Guardian* declared that " Liberal-Labour co-operation probably offers the only hope of preserving the country from another seven or eight years of Tory Government. But which Party will admit it ? "[29]

When the National Liberal Federation Council met in May 1934, however, its three leading spokesmen were hesitant, and inclined to point out the dangers involved in co-operation. Sir Herbert Samuel declared in favour of unity to defend " peace and freedom " with certain qualifications :[30]

If a powerful Government could be formed for those purposes that would be a great service to the nation and a real strengthening of its democratic institutions. But I am not willing to lend myself to the destruction of private enterprise and personal initiative, to transferring the whole of our industrial, commercial and financial system to political management.

Sir Archibald Sinclair declared his uncompromising opposition to going, " cap in hand ", to any other Party to " beg for existence " ; Liberals, he advised, should not wait at the Labour doorstep, but rather be working for progress and freedom. Mr Ramsay Muir claimed that any agreement with the Labour Party was " obviously impossible " because of the attitude of the Labour leaders ; by an alliance the Liberal Party would only " commit suicide ".

The Labour Party maintained the position it has consistently upheld since the war ; it would seek no alliances, but would concentrate all efforts on gaining a parliamentary majority. Both Morrison and Attlee announced there was no basis for agreement until the Liberals were prepared to accept socialism. Lansbury declared flatly, " There can be no sort of alliance between the Labour and Liberal Parties."[31] When, at a Liberal Summer School in 1934, a Labour candidate suggested a " reasonable understanding as to candidates ", the official organ of the Society of Labour Candidates denounced the proposal editorially under the title, " Compromising Candidates ".[32]

Mr Lloyd George's peace and reconstruction " New Deal " was viewed suspiciously by the Labour Party. Labour leaders likewise were very critical of the progressive programme proposed in a book, *The Next Five Years*, which was signed by more than a hundred persons of liberal sympathies.

Since the Liberals were overwhelmingly defeated in the 1935 Election, the problem of what will happen to their Party arises again, and it is a question of utmost importance to the future of the Labour Party. In the General Elections of 1922, 1923, 1924, and 1929, the Liberals held the balance of popular votes between the Labour Party and the Conservative Party. When frightened, the electorate has shown a marked tendency to shift from the Liberal candidates to Conservatives. This is indicated clearly in the Elections of 1924 and 1931, and to some extent explains the results of the 1935 Election.

It is a major problem of Labour strategy to win over the vast Liberal vote of the pre-1931 Elections. There is, however, a general sentiment within the Labour Party against any compromise on principles. The Liberal leaders are equally resolute. The argument is advanced that something akin to the French Popular Front might bring the Liberal and Labour Parties (at least) together into a successful joint electoral venture. It is overlooked frequently that the French and Spanish Popular Fronts were made necessary by a working class factionalized both politically and industrially. In Britain substantial political unity already exists in the Labour Party, and if present tendencies continue, the Liberal Party will pass from the scene.

The Labour Party still hopes to win over the Liberal voters to its Socialist programme, but a sudden crisis of great magnitude, precipitated by a fascist threat or war, might bring the remnants of Liberalism into an agreement with Labour on a limited programme of peace, social reform, personal freedom, and freer exchange of goods. Until then, Labour will seek no alliances, either of the " right " or " left ", but will concentrate on uniting the progressive forces within the Labour Party.

CHAPTER ELEVEN

REFERENCES

1 *A National Policy, An Account of the Emergency Programme advanced by Sir Oswald Mosley, M.P.* (London, 1931).

2 See John Strachey, *The Menace of Fascism* (London, 1933), pp. 163-5.

3 Sir Oswald Mosley, *The Greater Britain* (London, 1934), p. 28.

4 *Ibid.*, p. 26.

5 Clifford Allen, *Labour's Future at Stake* (London, 1932), pp. 16-47.

6 Lord Allen of Hurtwood, *Britain's Political Future, A Plea for Leadership and Democracy* (London, 1934), pp. 181-8.

7 Godfrey Elton, " A National Labour Party ? " *New Statesman and Nation*, Vol. iii (February 20th, 1932), pp. 221-2 ; Godfrey Elton, *Toward the New Labour Party* (London, 1932), pp. 14-18.

8 Godfrey Elton, *Toward the New Labour Party*, p. 42.

9 " National Government as a Political Method " in *Toward a National Policy, Being a National Labour Contribution* (London, 1935), p. 27.

10 " The Election and After ", in *The News Letter*, Vol. vii[i] (November 23rd, 1935), p. 73.

11 See *Budget Disclosure Inquiry, Report of the Tribunal Appointed under the Tribunals of Inquiry (Evidence) Act, 1921* (London, May 1936), pp. 23-4.

12 Egon Wertheimer, *Portrait of the Labour Party* (London, 1929), p. 18.

13 I.L.P., *Report of the Annual Conference, 1930*, pp. 82-3.

[14] J. Maxton, *Where the I.L.P. Stands* (London, 1930), p. 14.

[15] The story of I.L.P. disaffiliation may be traced in *The New Leader*, 1931 and 1932.

[16] I.L.P., *Report of the Annual Conference, 1932*, passim.

[17] The Conference is reported in : I.L.P., *Report of the Special National Conference held at Bradford, July 30th-31st, 1932*.

[18] See *Constitution and Rules of the I.L.P.*, as adopted at the Bradford Conference, 1932 ; *Report of the National Administrative Council of the I.L.P., for the Annual Conference, York, 1934*, pp. 16-19 ; I.L.P., *What the I.L.P. Stands For, 1935*.

[19] *New Statesman and Nation*, Vol. ix (May 18th, 1935), pp. 724.

[20] J. Maxton, *Lenin* (Edinburgh, 1932), p. 172 ; for the life story of this picturesque figure, see Gilbert McAllister, *James Maxton, Portrait of a Rebel* (London, 1934).

[21] *Railway Review*, January 13th, 1933 ; J. Compton, " The Unions, the Party, and the Breakaway I.L.P.", *Labour Magazine*, Vol. xi (September 1932), pp. 198-200.

[22] *Annual Report of the National Administrative Council to the Annual Conference of the I.L.P., Derby, 1935*, p. 6.

[23] C. K. Cullen, " The Revolutionary Policy Committee and the I.L.P.", *International Press Correspondence*, Vol. xv (November 9th, 1935), pp. 1457-8.

[24] *The R.P.C. Bulletin*, No. 23 (November 1935), pp. 2-3.

[25] C. K. Cullen, " Why We Broke with the I.L.P.", *Labour Monthly*, Vol. xvii (December 1935), pp. 741-6.

[26] Harry Pollitt, " The Seventh Congress of the Communist International ", *Labour Monthly*, Vol. xvii (October 1935), pp. 611-9.

[27] Lord Lothian, " Liberalism and Labour ", *New Statesman and Nation*, Vol. ix (April 27th, 1931), p. 583.

[28] *News Chronicle*, January 16th, 1933 ; *Gleanings and Memoranda*, Vol. lxxvii (February 1933), p. 147.

[29] *Manchester Guardian*, April 14th, 1934.

[30] *Ibid.*, May 5th, 1934.

[31] *Daily Herald*, May 7th, 1934.

[32] *Labour Candidate*, August-September 1934.

Chapter Twelve

SOCIALISM AND LABOUR PARTY TACTICS

A. The Party's Acceptance of Socialism

It is a commonplace observation that Britishers are averse to theorizing. They prefer rather to " muddle through ", seeking the methods which produce the best results, with appropriate deference to customs and traditions. This pragmatic characteristic is evident in the growth and development of the Labour Party. The Trade Unions, groping for better working conditions and higher wages, turned to political action and sought Labour representation in Parliament. Aided by Socialist groups in this endeavour, Trade Unionists listened to the fervent and eloquent propaganda of their new colleagues.

By 1918 the Party was ready to accept the mildly Socialist programme of Sidney Webb in *Labour and the New Social Order*, and to adopt a Constitution which stated as one of the Party's objects :

To secure for producers by hand and by brain the full fruits of their industry, and the most equitable distribution thereof that may be possible, upon the basis of common ownership of the means of production and the best obtainable system of popular administration and control of each industry and service.

The four points stressed in the 1918 declaration of policy were (1) the universal enforcement of an adequate national minimum standard of living, (2) the gradual socialization of the means of production, (3) taxation on the basis of ability to pay and the capital levy, and (4) the appropriation of surplus wealth for purposes of common good.

Labour and the Nation, the statement of aims approved by the Conference in 1928, pledged the Party on a number of Socialist plans, including nationalization of the Bank of England, coal, land, transport, power, and life insurance. *For Socialism and Peace*, which was adopted at the 1934 Conference, contains much of the same material, but brings it up to date and expands it with further detail.

Nearly all the leaders and a considerable proportion of the rank and file of the Labour Party consider themselves Socialists. But the designation means such different things to various people that it is necessary to examine in some detail the beliefs of leading groups. There are perhaps three main currents of ideas on policy in the Labour Party to-day.

B. SOCIAL REFORM : THE GOAL OF THE RIGHT-WING

The first group are Socialists in the Utopian sense only. They anticipate better conditions under a modified capitalist system, but would have the Party, when it achieves office, confine itself to legislation to improve wage standards, increase social services, and initiate other reforms. Mr C. T. Cramp, late General Secretary of the National Union of Railwaymen, threw light on the nature of this group's socialism in his statement :[1]

> In the main the Trade Unionist to-day is a Socialist. He does not quibble about academic points. He knows precious little about Karl Marx, but after listening to propaganda for many years he does believe that until the land, capital, resources, and skill of the people of this country are utilized for the people he will never obtain decent conditions.

The leaders of this group are chiefly Trade Unionists, and it is likely that their attitude is representative of the rank and file, to whom socialism " is hardly more than a genuine desire for improved conditions ".[2]

Mr Ernest Bevin in 1933 outlined a plan which might suit admirably as a programme of immediate social reforms for this group. It calls for the absorption of 2,000,000 unemployed by means of : (1) establishing a system of retirement pensions which are compulsory at sixty-five years of age and optional at sixty ; (2) providing disability pensions of one pound weekly for a single person and thirty-five shillings for man and wife ; (3) raising school leaving age to sixteen ; (4) reducing working hours to forty per week.[3]

The pressure on the next Labour Government to give its attention primarily to social reforms will be very great. Most of the responsible Trade Union leaders would advocate such a programme and it would be exceedingly difficult to resist. About one-third of the Members of a future Labour majority in the House of Commons will be financed by Trade Unions, assuming that the present system of financing candidates is continued, and that Trade Unions continue to finance about the same proportion of candidates they did in 1931 and 1935. Important matters of policy increasingly are decided by the National Council of Labour, on which there is a clear majority of Trade Union representatives. Moreover, the Trades Union Congress has expanded its authority to include consultation on all matters affecting the interest of Trade Unions—a very wide front.

All sections of the Party would agree that there is much which needs to be done forthwith to improve the condition of the working class. The nationalization of transport or coal mining probably will not lead to the reduction of unemployment ; indeed, government rationalization might push even more out of work. This necessity has been recognized, and matters of social reform have been given an important place in the Labour Party's programme.

The official Labour programme contains pledges to carry out many of the reforms demanded by the Trade Unionists. Its housing plans call for from 250,000 to 300,000 new houses per year. The Party has also declared for a socialized health service organized through local authorities, and for the continuance of the health insurance system with cash benefits only. Labour would raise the school-leaving age to sixteen, make secondary schools free, reduce the size of school classes, and provide University scholarships. Adequate maintenance of the unemployed would be made a national charge, and a huge public works programme would be launched.

The recent success achieved by French and American workers in securing measures of social amelioration has spurred British demands for immediate and tangible reforms. In Labour's Short Programme issued in March 1937, extensive improvements in the social services were projected, including most of the provisions of previous policy declarations. Among those stressed were the forty hour week, holidays with pay, abolition of the Means Test, retirement pensions, and others.

The chief objections which are raised to proceeding with a programme exclusively devoted to social reforms are : (1) that parliamentary time will be fully consumed by reformist measures, leaving no time for socialization legislation ; (2) that the limits beyond which taxation within the capitalist system will no longer produce revenue may be approached ; (3) that such a programme would be possible in a coalition or minority Government, which allegedly would be undesirable ; and (4) that many supporters of the Labour Party will withdraw unless Socialist measures are projected forthwith by the next Labour Government.

C. PIECEMEAL SOCIALIZATION : PROGRAMME OF THE MODERATE GROUP

A second group, for whom Herbert Morrison is the leading spokesman, wishes to concentrate major attention on legislation for the socialization of industry. Social reforms would not be completely overlooked, but would be pushed into the background, and the centre of the stage held by Labour's efforts to secure public control of the financial and economic apparatus of the country. Morrison claims that the test of the next Labour Government " is not primarily going to be : ' How much public money have you distributed ? ' but ' How many industries have you socialized ? ' "[4] His estimate is that two major industries can be socialized yearly.

The group takes a purely opportunist view of compensation, and apparently is willing to guarantee a rather high dividend to stockholders in order to secure voting rights. It holds that the essential thing is to obtain control of industry, and that the compensation basis can be adjusted later. It has been pointed out that this piecemeal nationalization may not improve the lot of the people unless it is co-ordinated through a planning agency.

Although Morrison and his followers do not have a distinct organized group through which they can advocate their programme of partial socialization, they have gathered support from nearly every element in the Party. The Trade Unionists have given their votes in Conference to make this the official Party policy, not realizing that it might conflict with their own demands on a Labour Government for immediate reforms. The opportunist elements in the Party support Morrison and the official programme.

D. Constitutional Revolution : The Demands of the Left-Wing

The third major stream of opinion in the Labour Party is expounded by a group of Socialists who stand considerably "left" of centre. They demand rapid and drastic socialization. Expecting opposition from the House of Lords, several in this group favour obtaining advance assurances from the Crown that sufficient peers will be created to make abolition of that House possible. They frankly say that a Labour Government which means business may have a financial crisis precipitated on it. Partial compensation only would be furnished to owners of socialized industries. Unlike their colleagues in the second category, many of the "left" prefer to discuss the eventuality of sabotage and unconstitutional resistance. It is possible that this outspokenness caused some losses at the polls in 1935, but some have justified the position on the grounds of intellectual honesty.

The leader and chief spokesman of this group is Sir Stafford Cripps ; many of the prominent "left" Labourites were united in the Socialist League. It acted as a "ginger" group within the Labour Party, urging it "left" and warning it to take a "realistic" view of the opposition which a Labour majority in the House of Commons must expect. The League had a membership of only about 2,000, but its rolls contained some of the most prominent names in the Movement. Besides Cripps, there were Sir Charles Trevelyan, once Labour President of the Board of Education, Professor Harold J. Laski, William Mellor, former editor of the *Daily Herald*, and others.

Dissolution of the Socialist League in 1937 leaves the "left" group without specific organizational leadership, but Cripps, Laski, and Pritt were elected to the Party Executive. They enjoy much confidence in the

Constituency Labour Parties, a majority of the votes of which usually are cast for " left " proposals in the Annual Conference.

Suspicious of the motives of the countries which dominate the League of Nations, many of this group have taken a stand against the use of sanctions. Some left-wing leaders have discussed with great frankness the possibility of assuming a temporary dictatorship and of curbing freedom of speech and press under certain conditions ; the programme may be described as " constitutional revolution ".

E.   CAN SOCIALISM COME BY DEMOCRATIC METHODS ?

Socialists of every country have long debated whether their aims can be achieved constitutionally, or whether they must resort to force. The Labour Party's traditional adherence to parliamentary action arises in part from both the flexibility of the British Constitution and the omnipotence of Parliament. The " inevitability of gradualness " philosophy taught the necessity of patient striving through regular constitutional channels. After the Russian Revolution, some Socialists left the Labour Party to join the Communists, but the number of such seceders has remained insignificant, and their revolutionary propaganda has affected the thinking of only a small fraction of British workers.

Disillusioned by the failure of the second Labour Government to make any considerable progress toward socialism and little toward social reform, many in the Labour Party began to reconsider its democratic aims. There was further cause for disquiet among Socialists who, during the " scare " campaign of 1931, recognized for the first time the fighting powers of the " dying capitalism ". Many were convinced by the quasi-constitutional rise to power of the German National Socialists that the reliance of Social Democrats on parliamentary action was not enough to cope with the great issues of a crisis. Nearly all groups within the Party, however, still expect that Labour's assumption of power will follow a victory at the polls.

F.   FORMATION OF A LABOUR GOVERNMENT

The Party has never committed itself against forming a minority or coalition Government, but sentiment within the Party remains hostile to such action. Moreover, the Co-operative Party has declared against participation unless there is a clear Labour–Co-operative majority. If the Co-operators adhere to this decision, Labour must have sufficient strength in Parliament to form a Government without Co-operative support. Some Labourites might support the formation of a minority Government which would introduce Socialist legislation and meet defeat at the outset, on the ground that such action would provide an auspicious platform from which to propagandize.

Under the procedure adopted by the 1933 Conference, the National Council of Labour, which consists of representatives from the National Party Executive, the Executive Committee of the Parliamentary Labour Party, and the General Council of the Trades Union Congress will convene after a successful Election and record its opinion on the advisability of the Labour

Party's assuming office.[5] Thus a joint recommendation of the three bodies represented may be secured. A minority Government would not be formed without first obtaining the approval of a special National Conference of organizations affiliated with the Party. In any case, the final decision still rests with the Parliamentary Party.

Because of unpleasant experiences with Mr MacDonald and the oligarchy which surrounded him, the Party has placed a number of restrictions on any future Labour Prime Minister and his Cabinet, designed to make them more responsible to the Parliamentary Party. Final responsibility for Ministerial appointments will continue to rest with the Prime Minister, who is Leader of the Party ; but he is to be advised and consulted by the Secretary of the Labour Party and three elected Members representing the Parliamentary Party. The Prime Minister is to be controlled by majority decisions of the Cabinet ; general financial policy is to be determined by the whole Cabinet, not by the Chancellor of the Exchequer alone. Dissolution may be ordered only by the decision of both the Cabinet and the Parliamentary Labour Party.

According to the policy outlined by the Conference, a Labour Government is to keep in touch with the Labour Movement as a whole, through three Cabinet Members who are to serve on the National Council of Labour. The relationship of the Government with the Parliamentary Party, which was a sore point in 1929-31, is to be maintained formally by a liaison

Minister and the Chief Whip, who are to attend the meetings of the Parliamentary Party's consultative committee. Ministers are expected to maintain informal contacts with back benchers, by consulting those who have training or experience in special fields. The Government is also directed to consult with the Trades Union Congress on any legislation directly concerning the industrial side of the Movement.

G.   Role of the Monarchy in the Socialist Transition

The Crown is an undemocratic institution, and as such it obviously would be out of place in the Socialist state desired by the Labour Party. There are good reasons, however, why the Party has avoided taking an official stand on the question, and why most Party leaders have not suggested a change in the Monarchy. First, George V, Edward VIII, and George VI, all have been popular with the electorate, and criticism might lead to severe repercussions at the ballot box. Second, the powers of the British Monarch are so limited by constitutional usage that the institution probably will provide no serious barrier to Socialist achievement. Third, the Party is staking much on the willingness of the Crown to create sufficient peers to clear the legislative tracks for the enactment of the Labour programme.

For these reasons and others, the Labour Party almost outdoes its rivals in expressing its loyalty to the King, and the *Daily Herald* gives its readers endless human interest stories on the Royal Family. Publicly,

Party leaders had nothing but praise for the late King George V, although many of them thought that he departed from the set constitutional practice in August 1931, in requesting Mr MacDonald to form a Coalition Government. Edward VIII received much laudation from Labourites. When the abdication crisis arose, no responsible Labourite advocated ending the Kingship.

The main controversy within the Party regarding the Monarchy concerns the appointment of peers. The official Party stand on the matter is that the King, being a constitutional monarch, will create peers according to the Government's recommendations. Professor Laski maintains that before taking office, the Party should obtain assurances from the Crown that such peers will actually be created,[6] just as such assurances were obtained by Lord Grey from William IV a century ago. If Labour has assumed office and the King " unconstitutionally " refuses to create the necessary peers, both Cripps and Laski argue that a revolutionary situation will exist.[7] This will compel either an immediate election on the single issue of the House of Lords, or, if this cannot be risked, possibly a temporary dictatorship might be assumed, or some other extra-constitutional action taken.

Laski has discussed the Monarchy with less reverence than other Party leaders, and has not hesitated to criticize the role George V played in the formation of the National Government in 1931[8] ; the accuracy of his description has since been substantiated by Dean Inge, the eminent churchman. According to

Dean Inge, when Mr MacDonald offered the King his resignation, the King refused and said :[9] " No, I don't want you to go. I want you to stay as trustee for the poor. Come back to-morrow morning and meet Mr Baldwin and Sir Herbert Samuel. Now go to bed."

Sir Stafford Cripps indiscreetly asserted in a public address in January 1934, that : " There is no doubt that we shall have to overcome opposition from Buckingham Palace and other places as well."[10]　This statement aroused a storm of criticism both within the Party and outside, although he explained later : " One always assumes the complete impartiality of the Crown in this country ", and that he meant only the court circles and hangers-on. Cripps' chief concern probably was to make it clear to both King and people that a Labour majority would be regarded as a mandate to take any necessary action to abolish the House of Lords.

At the time of the abdication crisis, the Parliamentary Labour Party supported the Government, chiefly on the grounds that Parliament must be supreme. Major Attlee criticized the glorification of Royalty and pled for geater simplicity.

H. Abolition of the House of Lords

There is general agreement within the Labour Party that the House of Lords must be abolished, both because it emphasizes the undemocratic class distinctions and because its conservative composition is an obstacle to Socialist legislation. The main problem

arises over the method of its extinction.   The official
programme of the Party pledges that a Labour Government meeting " sabotage " from the second chamber
would take immediate steps to overcome it, and " in
any event, during its term of office (will) pass legislation
abolishing the House of Lords as a legislative chamber."[11]
Although the Party has chosen to make only this
general statement, and to leave the exact method to
be determined by the circumstances, numerous
Labourites have ventured their individual opinions.

The left-wing group anticipates a crisis on Labour's
assumption of power, and both Laski and Cripps would
demand the immediate creation of sufficient peers to
act in the emergency, and then vote the Lords'
abolition.[12]   They feel that to delay the required two
years to pass legislation without the concurrence of the
Lords would be fatal ; it would, according to William
Mellor, " waste time, destroy confidence, and invite
sabotage ".[13]   Lord Ponsonby, while Labour Leader in
the second chamber, advocated the official Party plan
to adjust the method to the circumstances, claiming it
would be a tactical error to reveal in advance the exact
procedure to be followed.[14]

If a Conservative reform of the House of Lords is
carried out, the problem of the Labour Party may be
greatly complicated.   Such a scheme as was proposed
in 1932, for example, would confront a Labour majority
in the Commons with the " possible destruction of its
programme " by reconstituting the House of Lords
with important powers and an " eternal Tory
majority ".[15]

This proposal was made by an unofficial joint committee of Conservative Lords and Commoners, and would establish a reformed chamber of 320, of which 150 would be elected by proportional representation from and by the whole peerage, 150 elected by regions for twelve year terms, and the remainder made up of Princes of the Royal Blood, law Lords, and ecclesiastical authorities.

The failure of the National Government to push the reform is probably due to its recognition that, as a Conservative Member of Parliament has expressed it, " it is futile to imagine that any Upper House, especially one created *ad hoc* by a Party manœuvre, could resist the tidal wave of a left-wing majority in a newly elected House of Commons."[16]

I. REFORM OF THE HOUSE OF COMMONS PROCEDURE

It is sometimes said that the motives of Guy Fawkes in the " Gunpowder Plot " of 1605 may best be understood by visiting the House of Commons in session. The traditional procedure is so dilatory, involves so much repetition, and wastes so much parliamentary time that drastic reform will be necessary if a Government is to enact any considerable legislative programme. In making the case for revision of the House procedure, Dr Hugh Dalton has described its enervating atmosphere by saying : " Those who want to get things done, wilt ; those who want to get things said, luxuriate ; those who want neither, are not uncomfortable."[17] There are many, both within and outside the Labour Party, who believe the legislative machinery can be overhauled and improved without sacrificing any democratic principles.

The major reform which the Labour Party proposes to make in the House of Commons procedure concerns the key problem of time. It would establish a " time table " committee, probably representing the parties in proportion to their strength, which must allocate time for each stage of Government Bills beyond the first reading.[18] Committee work would be improved by increasing the number and decreasing the size of standing committees. Labour would simplify House procedure on financial business, which Dr W. Ivor Jennings has estimated takes over one-third of parliamentary time, by abolishing the special treatment accorded to financial resolutions, and treating fiscal legislation like any other Bills.

The Labour Party has declared that the work of Parliament ought to be confined to : (1) debating and deciding " the principles and general structure of legislation " ; and (2) examining and approving " orders and regulations issued by administrative departments to carry out legislation ".[19] Delegated legislation would be increased greatly, a step which the Party regards as necessary and inevitable because of the lack of time, technical complexities of legislation, and the need for flexibility. It is expected that wider use will be made of both Orders-in-Council and departmental regulations.

Probably due to the urging of the " left " group in the Party, the official statement of policy included a declaration concerning the action of a Labour Government if and when confronted with an emergency situation. Emergency powers would be sought from Parliament, and if the House of Lords resisted the crisis legislation, the Government would use : " all necessary powers in accordance with constitutional precedent ; and the Party would interpret its mandate from the electorate as conferring upon it full authority to proceed in this way."[19]

Even more fundamental changes in parliamentary procedure have been proposed. Cripps would combine a great amount of legislation into one yearly omnibus planning and finance Bill, and would handle details, major and minor, by administrative orders. Some secondary legislation would be dealt with by Parliament, but its role would be confined for the most part to the annual major Bill, and its committees, in reorganized form, would exercise general supervision over the Government's activities in their particular field.[20]

J. "DEMOCRACY VERSUS DICTATORSHIP"

The differences between the left-wing group and the more orthodox members of the Party over the general constitutional and political problems involved in the assumption of power are actually so small that it is surprising that one of Labour's most spectacular controversies should have arisen over them. Both sides want a Socialist programme and want it transformed into legislative terms. But Sir Stafford Cripps and the "left" group forsee trouble, and predict that attempts will be made to thwart the will of the people by economic manipulation and a barrage of propaganda from the capitalist press, or that the revision of the House of Lords may provide a permanent barrier to the achievement of Labour programme ; or that the anti-Socialists may resort to unconstitutional resistance. In any case, the former Socialist Leaguers would be prepared for appropriate action, constitutional or unconstitutional, to prevent the establishment of a dictatorship of the "right".

The chief Party leaders have chosen not to face these possibilities, but have preferred to uphold democracy generally, and to condemn with equal vehemence dictatorships of the "left" and "right". They take the opportunist view that bridges will be crossed when they are encountered, and that it is poor tactics to reveal to the enemy exactly how the Party will act under certain hypothetical situations. Sir Stafford Cripps and his colleagues maintained that it must be made clear to both people and King that the mandate asked for by the Party includes bold measures to meet any crisis which may arise.

CHAPTER TWELVE
REFERENCES

[1] *Labour Candidate*, February 1933, p. 4.

[2] J. Middleton Murry, " The Political Problem in Britain ", in *Marxism* (London, 1935), p. 188.

[3] Ernest Bevin, *My Plan for 2,000,000 Workless*, Clarion pamphlet (London, 1933) ; it appeared previously in the *New Clarion* from April 8th, 1933, to May 6th, 1933 ; the *New Clarion* for May 13th and May 20th, 1933, carried estimates on the cost of the plan by Colin Clark, lecturer on statistics at Cambridge University.

[4] Herbert Morrison, " Reform or Revolution ", *New Clarion*, Vol. vi (August 20th, 1932), p. 241.

[5] *1933 Conference*, pp. 8-10.

[6] Harold J. Laski, " Labour and the Constitution ", *New Statesman and Nation*, Vol. iv (September 10th, 1932), pp. 276-8.

[7] Sir Stafford Cripps, " Democracy and Dictatorship, the Issue for the Labour Party ", *Political Quarterly*, Vol. iv (October-December 1933), p. 472.

[8] Harold J. Laski, *The Crisis and the Constitution, 1931, and After* (London, 1932), pp. 31-6.

[9] W. R. Inge, D.D., " King George and His People ", *Evening Standard*, January 21st, 1936.

[10] *The Times*, January 6th, 1934.

[11] *For Socialism and Peace*, p. 31.

[12] Harold J. Laski, " Labour and the Constitution ", *New Statesman and Nation*, Vol. iv (September 10th, 1932), p. 276. Sir Stafford Cripps, *Can Socialism Come by Constitutional Methods?* issued by the Socialist League (1933), pp. 4-5 ; also in *Problems of a Socialist Government*, pp. 44-5.

[13] *Labour*, Vol. i (January 1934), p. 114.

[14] Lord Ponsonby, " The Farce of House of Lords Reform ", *Labour Magazine*, Vol. xi (December 1932), pp. 339-40.

[15] W. A. Rudlin, " Report on House of Lords Reform in Great Britain ", *American Political Science Review*, Vol. xxvii (April 1932), pp. 243-9.

[16] Hugh Molson, M.P., " The Future of the Constitution ", in *Conservatism and the Future* (London, 1935), p. 226.

[17] Hugh Dalton, *Practical Socialism for Britain* (London, 1935), p. 44.

[18] " Parliamentary Problems and Procedure ", in *1934 Conference*, p. 261.

[19] *Ibid.*, p. 263.

[20] Sir Stafford Cripps, *Can Socialism Come by Constitutional Methods?* pp. 7-11.

RECENT CONFLICTS OVER POLICY

A. AGENCY FOR THE MANAGEMENT OF SOCIALIZED INDUSTRIES

IT has long been the practice for Labour Party leaders to talk in rather vague terms about socialization, but to make no plans for dealing with the difficult problems of administration which this action would raise. During the second Labour Government, Herbert Morrison, Minister of Transport, and the late William Graham, President of the Board of Trade, began framing legislation to take over certain key industries. Morrison's first nationalization Bill reached the House of Commons before the fall of the Government, and was subsequently enacted in amended form by the National Government as the London Passenger Transport Act. He was also preparing legislation for the nationalization of both the electricity supply industry and the national transport industry, but it was cut short by the crisis of 1931. None of Graham's plans reached the stage of introduction in the House, but preparation of schemes for taking over the cotton and other industries aroused an interesting discussion within the Party.

The Party's vagueness about the methods of controlling socialized industries gave anti-Socialists an opportunity for attack. On one hand, they claimed that, by its lack of preparation, the Party demonstrated that it was unready to assume power ; on the other, they alleged that Socialists sought to bring all business under " political " control. Indeed, probably a majority of Labour leaders, if they have thought at all on the question, have assumed that management of future socialized industries would be placed in an appropriate department of the State, or turned over to the municipalities to administer. In their failure to suggest the possibility of using the public corporation, the mixed enterprise, and other forms of public control, Socialists overlooked the basis for a strong case which would meet many of their opponents' arguments about the inherent inefficiency or corruption involved in public ownership.

The public corporation idea, as expounded by Herbert Morrison, calls for the establishment in a particular socialized industry of a directing board appointed by the appropriate Minister on the basis of general ability. This board is to have full jurisdiction of the industry which it heads ; it is to determine day to day policy and to appoint the manager and staff. It is to be responsible to Parliament through the Minister, to whom Members may direct questions on the conduct of the industry. Ministers ordinarily lack both time and capacity to conduct the affairs of a great industry. Direct parliamentary responsibility might lead to ill-advised Election pledges, especially by candidates in preponderantly one-industry constituencies. Sponsors of this plan regard it as vitally necessary to have a semi-independent board of directors appointed for fixed terms.

The scheme has a general advantage in preserving the independence enjoyed by private business ; at the same time it eliminates private profits and makes central planning possible. The chief controversy over socialization schemes has raged over compensation and workers' representation, but several Socialists have attacked the idea of having a highly paid board when the goal of the Party is a classless society. Advocates of the plan reply that, in the initial stages, socialized industries must compete with capitalist enterprise in obtaining managerial material of ability, and that it would be foolish to risk the success of a nationalized industry by appointing persons of inferior calibre to be in charge of it.[1]

The advocates of the public corporation do not claim that it is the best form of organization for all types of socialized ventures. Municipalization will be used for certain functions ; retail Co-operatives may assume responsibility for distribution ; the Post Office will probably continue as a departmentally administered service, and other routine functions may be handled in the same way. To assume, as spokesmen for the Union of Post Office Workers apparently have done, that all forms of organization for public business except those employing direct parliamentary responsibility are bad, is unduly dogmatic. Technical and minute problems in the cotton, railway or coal businesses are best dealt with by a small body of skilled persons who devote most of their time to the particular industry.

It may be said that the public corporation idea is the one most widely accepted in the Labour Party to-day, but Party leaders are largely in agreement that the form of organization for a particular industry should be decided on its merits. Two safeguards appear necessary if the plan is to be successful—the public corporation must bow to the authority of a national planning agency, and must be subject to adequate parliamentary control.

B. COMPENSATION OF FORMER OWNERS OF INDUSTRY

The problem of compensation aroused a great controversy in the Labour Party during the framing of the Party's present policy statement. It is obvious to most British Labourites that some form of remuneration is necessary if the transition to socialism is to be achieved peacefully. Since the Party has adopted a policy of piecemeal socialization, confiscation or even less than full compensation would work injustice to certain groups of owners who have investments in the particular industries slated for early nationalization. "Why favour", asks Dr Dalton, "the investor in a boot factory, a rubber plantation, a diamond mine or a night club . . . as against the investor in a railway or a colliery company?" There is also the very practical consideration that ownership in industry is too widely spread in the middle class and certain sections of the working class to make confiscation, whole or partial, politically a possibility.

The problem facing the Labour Party is not to decide between compensation and confiscation, but rather to determine a basis for compensation. The policy adopted by the 1932 Conference in " National Planning of Transport " and that approved by the 1934 Conference in " Public Ownership and Compensation ", embody the formula used by Morrison in the original London Transport Bill, called " reasonable net maintainable revenue ". Under this scheme consideration is given to (1) average net profits for the three years preceding socialization, (2) the probability that such profits would have been earned if private ownership continued, and (3) direct pecuniary losses sustained by socialization. No consideration is granted to (1) possible future advantages of amalgamation, (2) possible increased value under public ownership, or (3) the compulsory nature of the purchase.[2] Simply stated, Mr Morrison proposes that the regular earnings of the stock and bondholders of industry, if " reasonable ", shall continue (or be paid off). The question as to whether the owners of an industry which is being socialized should be paid in cash or securities in the public enterprise (without voting rights) is largely one of expediency, and the decision will depend upon the conditions prevailing at the time of the transfer. It is likely that the former owners will be given shares in the public enterprise, thereby avoiding the necessity for issuing new stock or floating a large loan.

Although the above policy of quite full compensation was adopted by large majorities in two Conferences, some strong opposition appeared to the Morrison proposals, chiefly from leaders identified with the Socialist League. In place of " net reasonable maintainable revenue ", this group proposed as a basis of compensation the provision of income allowances for a period of years, but no capital repayment except for certain funds and in cases of individual hardship. They maintained that the payment of interest over a period of years plus the eventual repayment of the capital constitutes an unbearable burden on the industry, and creates a perpetual rentier class which can live on its investments in socialized industries.[3] Rejecting the Executive's arguments for the Morrison formula, Sir Stafford Cripps summed up the case of the " left " group :[4]

If we are really going out for a planned Socialist State we have definitely to take up the point of view that the capital value of industries has been created by the workers of this country, and they are not going to pay for them when they take them back into their own ownership.

Although their amendment for terminable annuities and no capital repayment was rejected by the Conference, the Socialist League group managed to secure interesting statements from advocates of the official plan.

The official declaration states that fortunes may be levelled down by the taxation of incomes and inheritances ; both the policy statement and Morrison's speech at the 1934 Conference stress the point that the burden of interest cannot be carried for ever, but both are equally indefinite as to what will be done about it. Driving home the demand that Labour get on with the job of socialization, Morrison said in part :[5]

Put us in that position (a parliamentary majority and a few great industries socialized).   Let a Labour Government go on with its work of socialization. Make us substantially economic masters of the State. Remove capitalist control over the great field of industry. Then is the time to take the big decision, which I assure you I personally should not be afraid to take, when this country has become a substantially socialized country. The burden of capital interest must stop, the settlement of accounts be commenced, and then we can make a fair, a clean, and an equitable sweep. . . .

Sir John Simon's interpretation as to what Morrison meant by the " big decision " is probably not far from the truth ; a measure of confiscation or scaling down of capital would take place. In essence, then, Cripps and Morrison may have meant much the same thing, namely, that annuities should be paid through the transition period. Cripps chooses to say at the outset that he means to eliminate all rights to capital repayment ; Morrison, thinking of the next Election and of getting popular support for his socialization plans, wishes to pay regular interest and to " adjust " the capital at an opportune later moment. Such difference between the two men occurs repeatedly.[6]

C. WORKERS' REPRESENTATION

The second major controversy over the socialization of industry concerned the right of organized workers to have a voice in management. The claims arose from two sources ; Trade Unionists in industries likely to be taken over demanded participation in control on the grounds that they were forced to give up certain other rights when an industry became public ; and a group of Socialists, chiefly of the guild school, claimed workers' control was an indispensable step toward industrial democracy. Mr Morrison resisted the claims of both, first in the London Transport scheme, and later in the framing of general Party policy. But the combination of some powerful Trade Unionists and some Labour intellectuals forced the Executive to include in *For Socialism and Peace* the following : " The Labour Party also believes that the employees in a socialized industry have a right, which should be acknowledged by law, to an effective share in the control and direction of the industry."

The case against workers' control was ably advanced by Morrison, with the backing of the Executive.[7] First, he argued, it is desirable that the Minister or other appointing authority should have a free hand to select an efficient governing board wholly on the grounds of ability. Second, if any " sectional " interests are granted representation, all will demand it. Third, the Labour representative on the board would have an exceedingly difficult role, because most Trade Unionists in the industry would be concerned chiefly with their own immediate surroundings or workshop, make demands accordingly, and neglect the larger aspects of the whole. Finally, he cites Soviet Russia's experience with workers' control and her abandonment of it.

The demands for workers' control are derived from earlier propaganda efforts of the syndicalists, the guildists, and the shop stewards movement. More recently, they have been eloquently voiced by Mr H. E. Clay, as Secretary of the Passenger Transport Division of the Transport and General Workers' Union and Chairman of the London Labour Party. Among the arguments for a measure of participation by Labour in management, Clay enumerated : (1) the workers are not content to be " the hewers of wood and the drawers of water under the perpetual control of their bosses ", but demand free citizenship in an industrial democracy ; (2) Labour representatives have an understanding of certain phases of industrial life which will enable them to make a very real contribution to management ; (3) Labour is not a sectional interest but an organic part of industry on which the whole productive structure rests.[8]

The extent of worker participation in management demanded by advocates of the cause is rather limited. Mr Clay asked the 1932 Conference to approve only a minor amendment to the transport policy statement, declaring that the Minister should appoint the board of the socialized services after consultation with the Trade Unions involved. Both the report and the amendment were withdrawn for further consideration. In 1933, a more extensive and general declaration was made over Executive opposition on the motion of the National Union of General and Municipal Workers, claiming for workers an effective share of the control and direction of socialized industries. The big Unions split about evenly on the issue, and it was carried by the votes of the local Labour Parties and Socialist societies.

Even Morrison agreed that there should be a full measure of consultation with workers in factory and workshop, but he was not prepared to allow representation of any group as such on the governing body. The advocates of representation argued, with much justice, that some special interests would be represented whether the basis for appointment was ability or otherwise. They pointed out that the lack of workers' representation, combined with other features of Morrison's public corporation, and the perpetuation of the interest-drawing class, made the socialized industry little improvement over its capitalist predecessor. Both Cole and Cripps have insisted that workers' participation in management must be limited to the details of working conditions, and that the Government planning agency must have full authority over prices and production.[9]

D. Problems in the Socialization of Particular Industries

Most Socialist writers advocate that the Labour Party's initial step on assuming power should be to take over banking and financial institutions, which they regard as the key of British economic life. The Party proposes to establish three chief agencies in the field, the public Bank of England, a single banking corporation combining all joint-stock banks, and a new national investment board with power to license and direct investment and to mobilize financial resources.

The Executive's policy proposal did not include taking over the joint-stock banks, but it suffered one of its rare Conference defeats on this issue in 1932. The case of the Executive against the amendment to

socialize joint-stock banks was that sufficient consideration had not yet been given to this action. Sir Stafford
Cripps and E. F. Wise, in support of such an amendment, claimed the control of banking was so vital to
the whole Socialist plan that these important financial
institutions should not be omitted. The Conference
ordered their inclusion. The Party has declared that
the aim of British monetary policy should be to
" stabilize wholesale prices at suitable level in this
country ", and to seek foreign exchange stability by
international agreement. Labour's Immediate Programme, issued recently, omits reference to the joint-
stock banks, but states that the gold standard should
not be restored.

Coal mining is the most distressed industry in
Britain, and both the acuteness of its condition and the
power of the mineworkers within the Labour Party will
make for its early nationalization. British supplies of
electric power and gas are both largely dependent upon
coal. So important is the industry and so chaotic its
condition that the National Government has announced
forthcoming legislation nationalizing coal royalties.

The arguments in favour of transport co-ordination
are also extremely strong, for both railway and road
transport services are definitely lacking in planned
development and require immediate attention. The
Labour Party proposes to set up a national transport
board with powers to take over the railways and other
major services at once, and to plan for the nationalization of air, waterway, and other services at a later
date.[10]

Some progress has already been made in the central planning of electricity supply under the Electricity Supply Acts of 1919 and 1926 and through the agencies created by them, namely, the Electricity Commission which co-ordinates supply undertakings on a regional basis, and the Central Electricity Board, which provides similar services on a national basis. Labour's programme calls for the establishment of a national electricity board with power to take over all existing governmental functions, including the national grid which transports electricity, and privately owned plants as fast as it deems desirable. Gas enterprises were included among the industries listed for early socialization in Labour's Short Programme.

As the first step in reorganizing British agriculture, the Labour Party proposes to bring land under public ownership. Not only is this step important to agriculture, but it is regarded as basic for Socialist planning. A general enabling act would give the Government power to acquire land and set the basis for compensation. A national agricultural commission would supervise land utilization, production, and marketing. The Short Programme does not call for nationalization of the land, except for immediate public uses.

Banking, mining, transport, electricity, land—these have been designated by the Party for early socialization. A middle group of industries, iron and steel, cotton, heavy engineering, building and motor, are likely to follow. Distribution and foreign trade, because of the important role played by the Co-operative Movement, will probably be among the last to require socialization.

E.   The Collective Security System

The most outstanding achievements in the two Labour Governments were in the field of international relations. Like other Socialist parties, Labour anticipates the eventual coming of a world Socialist commonwealth and the " brotherhood of man ".   The Party is not officially pacifist, but it recognizes that keeping the peace now may be the only hope of avoiding catastrophe, and is an essential pre-requisite to the international socialism to which it aspires.   Its chief policy in foreign affairs, therefore, is based on the erection of a strong collective peace system, through the League of Nations, seeking the fulfilment of treaty obligations under the Kellogg-Briand Pact.

To the majority in the Party, the key to successful collective action to maintain peace is the readiness of the country to take such steps, economic or military, as are necessary to halt an aggressor nation.   The Party also is committed to propose a plan for drastic multilateral disarmament, including the abolition of national air forces, and the internationalization of civil aviation, items which are stressed in the recent Short Programme.   Labour seeks to abolish the private manufacture of armaments.   Ultimately, the Party hopes for the establishment of an international police force under League authority.

Opposition to the official policy comes from several quarters.   Lord Ponsonby, and other ardent pacifists, stood for unilateral " disarmament by example " and maintained that the perpetuation of force in international affairs through an international police force was both undesirable and impracticable. The Socialist League point of view, expressed by William Mellor and others, was that because war is a product of capitalism, and because capitalist countries will not surrender enough sovereignty to make peace possible, a Labour Government's foreign policy should be based on joint action with the U.S.S.R. and other Socialist countries.

F. THE CONTROVERSY OVER SANCTIONS

Both the pacifist and the Socialist League groups were involved in the sanctions controversy of 1935, which seriously divided the Party just before the General Election. The chief leaders of both groups lined up against the Executive's proposals for invoking economic sanctions against Italy, and vacated their Party offices when the Conference decided to support the Executive recommendation. The policy adopted provided first for sanctions to halt the Italo-Abyssinian war, and second urged the League of Nations to call a world economic conference to set up an international control of raw materials. Dr Dalton described this policy as " pooled security plus pooled plenty ", and it received the eloquent support of a majority of Labour's leaders. Lord Ponsonby, George Lansbury, Dr Alfred Salter, and others, adopted the consistent pacifist view that the use of force could not be justified, and claimed that sanctions, effectively applied, might mean war.

The case put forward by the Socialist Leaguers who opposed sanctions, was based on less consistent and

more complex grounds.   Cripps frankly stated that he
had altered his position within the last few months,
that he was satisfied the League of Nations had become
the "tool of satiated imperialist powers" and an
"International Burglars' Union".[11]   Mellor pointed
out the dangers involved in supporting the Executive
report, claiming that "economic sanctions involve the
use of military force . . .", that the League Covenant
was the "sheet-anchor of British imperialism", and
that security "in this world conflict (of imperialism)
within capitalism is sheer impossibility".[12]

G.   Labour and the Empire

The Labour Party is definitely anti-imperialistic and
very critical of the methods used to build up the
British Empire.   But it hopes that the unity of the
"British Commonwealth of Nations" may be
preserved, with each as a free and equal partner, for
the purpose of "leading the world along the way to an
international federation, within which the strong
nations would cease to exploit the weak . . ." and
each exerting its influence for peace.[13]   Labour
Conferences repeatedly have declared for self-government and self-determination of the Indian people.

In the backward colonies, Labour has pledged to
resist "capitalist exploitation", and has promised to
employ its "doctrine of trusteeship", which involves
the subordination of every other consideration to the
welfare of the native populations.   It has been
recognized by the Party that many of the colonies are
incapable of self-government in the near future, and

that British evacuation might leave the natives as prey for buccaneers and other powers.

A future Labour Government may be embarrassed seriously by colonial problems. On one hand, reports of native dissatisfaction or violence may cause dissention at home. On the other, foreign " have not " powers may use the opportunity to press their claim for a greater share of colonial possessions.

H. The Present International Dilemma

In the last two years the Labour Party has faced an increasingly difficult international situation. The Fascist bloc is menacing ; the Rome-Berlin-Tokio axis is strengthened ; Italy took Ethiopia ; Spain and China may yet be taken or partitioned ; Fascist armaments cast an ominous shadow over West and East ; the League of Nations has lost prestige and strength.

What can the Labour Party do under these circumstances ? Mr Lansbury and a small group would have the Party accept their pacifist attitude, consistently refuse to take part in the mad arms race, and seek all means of peaceable settlement. The "left" group, led in part by former Socialist Leaguers, regards the struggle with Capitalism, especially in its acute Fascist form, as all important, and continues to advocate an agreement with France, U.S.S.R. and other powers under left control.

The Party's majority, however, has leaned toward the National Government's policies in regard to Spain and rearmament. For a time, the Party supported

" non-intervention " in the Spanish Civil War. Trevelyan, Addison, Noel-Baker, and others at the 1936 Conference made out a strong case for the rights of the Spanish Government to buy arms, but the Conference voted support of " non-intervention " by a large majority, holding that the risks of war were too great. By 1937, however, the " non-intervention " policy was so generally regarded as a snare and a delusion that the Conference unanimously adopted Trevelyan's resolution calling for an end to " non-intervention " and sponsoring the Spanish Government's international rights. Already the Party Executive and the National Council of Labour had changed, and, perhaps too late, Spain's Popular Front Government was given the support it has long merited from social democratic movements everywhere. Major Attlee and many other prominent Labourites have visited Spain and encouraged the war-weary Loyalists : the Labour and Co-operative Movements are raising funds for food and medical supplies.

The British rearmament programme, unlike the Government's Spanish policy, attracted the early hostility of Labourites, but the Party majority gradually has accepted it as a necessity. In 1936 the Party withheld support from the Government's arms plan ; in 1937 the Parliamentary Party decided not to vote against final estimates for military services ; the 1937 Conference followed the Trades Union Congress and overwhelmingly adopted the National Council of Labour's policy statement, endorsing rearmament. Considerations of *macht politik* have thrown Tory imperialists into the anti-Fascist camp ; Labourites, recognizing the dangers of Italian, German, and Japanese aggression, find themselves in agreement with the Conservatives on rearmament.

The Party continues, in its Short Programme, to restate its earlier policies of collective security to be attained through League action. It supports an international air police force and would internationalize civil aviation. Labour's much controverted new stand on armaments is explained in terms of Britain's obligations to the League and to the British Commonwealth of Nations.

CHAPTER THIRTEEN

REFERENCES

1 Exposition of the public corporation idea is found in Herbert Morrison, *Socialization and Transport* (London, 1933), pp. 131-88 ; Thomas Johnston, former Lord Privy Seal, maintains that " useful and necessary " steps towards socialism can be taken through this medium, *Forward*, July 8th, 1933 ; criticisms are voiced by H. N. Brailsford in his article " Nationalization ", *New Clarion*, Vol. i (October 29th, 1932), p. 491, and by others in letters to the editor, *Ibid.* (September 17th, 1932), p. 357.

2 Herbert Morrison, *op. cit.*, pp. 256-9.

3 Harold J. Laski, " We Seek a Society of Equals ", *New Clarion*, Vol. i (September 3rd, 1932), p. 295.

4 *1934 Conference*, p. 194.

5 *Ibid.*, p. 199.

6 See Ernest Davies, " We Must First Compensate Then Confiscate ", *New Nation*, Vol. ii (December 1934), pp. 133-4 ; Sir Stafford Cripps, " The Prospect for Britain ", III, *New Nation* (November 1934), pp. 123, 128. Mr Morrison also wrote : " This party is not for confiscation. I am clear that the burden of interest cannot go on for ever. Somehow, at the right time, a substantially socialized society will get rid of it. In the meantime I agree with Trotsky : ' Compensation or confiscation is largely a matter of expediency.' " *New Clarion*, Vol. i (September 17th, 1932), p. 357.

7 See Herbert Morrison, *Socialization and Transport*, pp. 189-242 ; *1932 Conference*, pp. 211-40. Morrison once wrote that " this buses for the busmen and dust for the dustmen stuff is not socialism at all." It is,

he claimed, " middle-class syndicalist romanticism."
New Clarion, Vol. i (September 17th, 1932), p. 357.

8 See Dalton, *op. cit.*, p. 164 ; A. Creech Jones, " The
Problem of Workers' Control ", *New Clarion*, Vol. ii
(February 11th, 1933), p. 192 ; J. E. D. Bradfield,
" What Morrison Doesn't Want ", *Socialist Review*,
Vol. v (January 1934), pp. 39-45 ; Harold E. Clay,
Workers' Control, Socialist League, Forum Lecture
Series, No. 8 (1933) ; reprinted in *Problems of a Socialist
Government* (London, 1933), pp. 209-28 ; Harold E.
Clay, "The Workers' Voice in Industry", *New Clarion*,
Vol. ii (May 27th, 1933) p. 391 ; *Ibid.* (June 3rd,
1933), 413.

9 Sir Stafford Cripps, " The Prospect for Britain ", *New
Nation*, Vol. ii (October 1934), p. 111.

10 See Herbert Morrison, *Socialization and Transport*,
pp. 61-104 ; Hugh Dalton, *op. cit.*, pp. 117-28 ;
National Planning of Transport, Labour Party, November
1932, pp. 11-16.

11 *1935 Conference*, pp. 157-8.

12 *Ibid.*, pp. 170-2.

13 George Lansbury, *Labour's Way With the Commonwealth*
(London, 1935), pp. 90-1.

PART V
CONCLUSION

Chapter Fourteen

AN APPRAISAL

A. Assets and Liabilities of the Labour Party

The Labour Party is an admirable organization, unique in many ways among the major parties of all countries. The amount of enthusiastic volunteer work done without expectation of personal reward is remarkable. The Labour vote-getting machinery, considering the cause to which it is devoted, perhaps surpasses in effectiveness the most highly perfected American political machines sustained by spoils.

Democratic financing has been approached by building up an extensive dues paying membership, individual and affiliated, and by placing little or no reliance on large contributions by wealthy individuals. Leadership of the Parliamentary Party is mainly in the hands of intelligent and well-trained men and women. On the whole, Labour Members of Parliament and local office holders maintain discipline and provide genuine Party responsibility. The episodes of 1931 demonstrated that Labour's minimum strength in the country is nearly one-third of the electorate ; the Party is rooted in the bed rock of British Trade Unionism.

Many criticisms of the Labour Party have been motivated by tactical and ideological differences ; organizational features rarely have been judged on their merits. There is considerable validity in the charge that it is a sectional Party, dominated structurally by a single organized economic interest. A majority in the country is middle-class in its thinking, if not in income ; certainly the organized sectors of the working class constitute a minority in the electorate. Trade Union supremacy has curtailed and frustrated the local Labour Parties, which, even after the 1937 reforms, are given an inadequate voice in Party affairs. Financial resources available for the political purposes of the Labour and Co-operative Movements are unevenly and unenlightendly spread, if the goal is the achievement of a powerful Labour Government. Disciplinary powers sometimes have been used in a manner which has tended to stifle independent thinking in the Party. Deviation to the " left " of the Party line is apt to lead to heresy hunting, but little attention is given to the effects of the " aristocratic embrace " on the " right."

B. The Trade Unions and the Labour Party

Many contradictory opinions have been advanced concerning the role of Trade Unions in the Labour Party's structure. Paul Blanshard, present Commissioner of Accounts in New York City, wrote in 1923 that : " The trade unions are in such complete control of the Labour Party that they could not stomach any political leaders who were not in complete sympathy with their views."[1] A year later Fred Bramley, then Secretary of the Trades Union Congress, declared :[2]

The political progress of the Labour Party . . . is mainly trade union political progress. . . . The political organization is kept running by trade union funds, and the Political Labour Party in this Country can be referred to as a Trade Union Labour Party, if we wish to use that term.

In 1925, Professor R. H. Tawney was able to tell an American audience that after 1918, while Trade Union membership in the Labour Party was maintained, " the balance of power was shifted from them to the local Labour Parties. . . ."[3] Although local Parties have grown steadily since that time, events of the late twenties (particularly the General Strike) checked this tendency, and the crisis of 1931 was the occasion for its reversal.

Determined not to permit the Labour politicians to get out of hand again, the Trade Unions reasserted their dominant power in the Party Conferences and on the Executive. In addition, they obtained a new strength by amending the composition of the National Council of Labour to give the T.U.C. representatives a clear majority over those of the Party and the Parliamentary Labour Party. The joint body then undertook to frame policy on all questions affecting the Labour Movement as a whole, and to provide for united action in case of a national emergency. An increasing number of important decisions is being made by the National Council of Labour, and, if Conference decrees are adhered to, crucial questions on the formation and conduct of a Labour Government will be reviewed by the joint agency.

It is surprising that the Labour Party has retained its original federal structure representing interest groups nationally. The framework savours of the

20

temporary ; it might well have been dropped in 1918
with the expansion of local Labour Parties. Labour's
" Federal Alliance " yields a sort of disproportionate
functional representation, a lop-sided " parliament of
industry " within the Party structure. All this is quite
contrary to the usual type of Party organization which,
like legislative bodies over most of the world, is based on
geographical areas. Consider the protests which
would emanate from Labour sources if the Conservative
Party reorganized its machinery, openly giving majority
power over structure and policy to employers'
associations and like groups !

Doubtless the recent concessions granted to local
Parties will relieve much tension and dissatisfaction
within the ranks of Labour. Further concessions may
be made by setting up an official national association
of Constituency Parties, and by pooling Conference
expenses or allowing proxy voting. The Movement,
however, may do well to face up with certain more
fundamental reforms which would solve several of the
Party's outstanding problems.

C. Proposals for Reform

1. *Reorganization of the Party on a Constituency Basis.*
This move would involve rebuilding the National Party
to include only Constituency Labour Parties. The
Trade Unions and Socialist societies now affiliated
nationally would be invited to affiliate their members
locally with the appropriate Constituency Parties. All
affiliation fees should be paid to local Parties, which
would forward a portion to the Central Office. Some

formula should be found whereby Constituency Parties might differentiate fairly between affiliated members and individual members, providing representation for them with due regard for their different contributions, in both funds and Party work.

The barriers to such a reorganization are very great. The withdrawal of income from national affiliation fees might cripple temporarily the work of the Central Office. Some Trade Unions might sever their Party connections altogether. These considerations and others would cause most Labourites to assert that such a reform cannot be carried through a Conference.

But the advantages of reorganization must not be overlooked. Validity to the charge that Labour is structurally a sectional Party largely would be eliminated. Constituency Parties would be given authority commensurate with the responsibility which they already bear ; this change would add immeasurably to the morale and effectiveness of local groups. Chosen to represent them, the Executive and Conference would be keenly sensitive to Labour's position in the constituencies, where, after all, the battle for National power is being fought. New impetus to participate in local Party affairs would be given to individual Trade Unionists. Members of many Co-operative societies already affiliated locally might be brought into full Party membership.

2. *Financing Parliamentary Candidates Only by Divisional Parties*. This reform is essential to eliminate the division of loyalties of Labour M.P.s and to spread equitably the resources of the Movement. The

organizationally financed M.P. owes a major obligation to his sponsoring group, rivalling that to constituents and Party. It has been shown above that in contested constituencies in the 1935 Election, Trade Union and Co-operative Party candidates spent on the average nearly twice as much as those financed by Divisional Labour Parties. The results of the present system may be seen on Labour's parliamentary back benches—a handful of M.P.s under forty years, and a large group beyond middle age.

In addition, the individual contributions of well-to-do candidates must be curbed rigidly. The present method of financing places a premium on the prospective candidate with financial backing, and operates against one with more ability and training but lacking both personal wealth and organizational sponsorship. The Constituency Party is weakened by overspending on the part of the candidate.

The existing restrictions imposed by the Party already have strained Labour–Co-operative relationships. This reform might precipitate a major crisis between the two Parties. If Constituency Labour Parties are to retain their virility, however, present safeguards must be maintained and extended. Eventually the Co-operative Movement must decide whether to pool its political resources with the Labour Party or to withdraw from Party politics altogether. A successful independent Co-operative Party appears outside the realm of possibility.

3. *Equal Representation on the National Council of Labour.* During recent years the freedom of the Party

and the Parliamentary Party has been curtailed greatly by this joint body's increasing authority over policy. Certainly no Council policy announcements should be made until each organization's executive approves. By all means, the Parliamentary Party must not be committed by the T.U.C. majority on the National Council of Labour.

It must not be forgotten that the Labour Party owes its very existence to the Trade Unions, which generously have provided strength, succour and stability. Proposals for changing the existing relationship between the Party and the Unions need not arise from ingratitude on the political side, but rather from the point of view of the full grown and ambitious youth who, with the blessing of his parent, goes forth to seek his bride—an electoral majority.

As this is written, the outlook for the Labour Party is the brightest since 1931. The Bournemouth Conference of 1937 may be looked upon in future years as a turning point in Labour history, marking a revival of morale and the reunion of elements within the Party after long internecine warfare.

If the present unity and confidence persist, doubtless the outstanding problems of the Labour Party will be solved with the same spirit of conciliation which attended the recent organizational reforms. Meanwhile the campaign for power centres around the Immediate Programme and may yet lead to the formation of a third Labour Government.

Chapter Fourteen

REFERENCES

[1] Paul Blanshard, *An Outline of the British Labour Movement* (New York, 1923), p. 28.

[2] Fred Bramley, " The Trades Union Congress ", in Richard W. Hogue (ed.) *British Labour Speaks* (New York, 1924), p. 81.

[3] R. H. Tawney, *The British Labour Movement* (New Haven, 1925), p. 35.

INDEX